HITTING THE BALL
YOU CANNOT SEE

JURIE KRIEL

& THE NXT MOVE COMMUNITY

CONTENTS

INTRODUCTION
HITTING THE BALL YOU CANNOT SEE

PART 1
HOW WE LIVE (EXPERIENTIAL)

PART 2
HOW THE WORLD WORKS (STRUCTURAL)

PART 3
HOW WE CONNECT (RELATIONAL)

CONCLUSION
GOD IS IN OUR FUTURE

ACKNOWLEDGEMENTS

"Creativity is forgetting where you got it from."

Bear with me as I try to remember. The ideas and concepts within this book are not only my own, but rather a collection of seeds planted and nurtured by countless individuals in my life. I am convinced that what is presented here as my original thought has been shaped by the grace of God working through you. I pray that I have been a good steward of it.

Firstly, thank you to the dearest person on earth to me, my wife, Karin Kriel. You are the love of my life and my greatest co-conspirator in the gospel and I'm grateful to walk this journey with you. To my children who have taught me more than I could ever teach you, may you hit a home run in your generation. To my parents and siblings, thank you for bearing and causing the chaos with me. The love, support, and patience provided by each of you have been a constant source of strength.

To every teacher, youth leader, pastor, lecturer, congregation member, co-worker, and friend—each of you have played a role in my journey. You have taught me, challenged me, and inspired me. If the seeds you planted are now bearing any fruit or if they inspire a new seed in a reader's life, you have a part in that harvest.

This book would not exist without the dedication and hard work of the team that directly assisted me. A heartfelt "Thank you!" to Cheryl Meredith-Krueger, Ulrich Lombard, Olinka Smit, Kasey Hatfield, Lisa van der Walt and Sherri Breaux. Your tireless efforts in researching, collating, editing, organizing, designing and refining this manuscript were invaluable. Those reading have no idea what a mess it would have been without you. There is no way this book could have happened without you.

I am deeply grateful to Jason Hatfield and Matthew Niermann. Your benevolent and generous sharing of thoughts and resources have shaped this book more than any of its readers will ever know. Your hearts and minds shaped this conversation. Matthew, your initial writing shaped so much of what would follow.

To the entire Shoreline Church family, staff team, and our pastors, Rob and Laura Koke—thank you for inspiring and exemplifying so much of what is contained in these pages. Your ministry and investment in us have blessed us immeasurably, and by extension, every person who reads this book will be impacted.

A special note of thanks to Mac Pier, Samuel Chiang, Michael Oh, Dave Bennett, and Michael A. Ortiz. Thank you for trusting me, inviting me to speak and collaborate in the facilitation of think tanks, conversations, conferences, and congresses that, in a very big way, informed the understanding and skills contained in this book. Your trust and partnership allowed me to engage with global Christian leaders and glean the insights that form the very backbone of this work.

To every one of the thousands of participants and delegates, every person that filled out a survey, contributed to a group discussion, answered questions on mentimeter or contributed to one of the many focus groups— I pray that we have represented your input well in this book.

Finally, to the NXT Move community (it is so hard to not list each of you by name), and particularly to those who were interviewed in the writing of this book: your amazing work for the Kingdom inspires me daily. Though I know I am not worthy of tying any of your sandals, I am deeply grateful to share life and the driving passion to see Jesus-following excel for generations to come. To every one of you, may Christ in you shine through me and this book to everyone that reads it.

INTRODUCTION
THE BALL YOU CANNOT SEE

WHEN WE'RE BUSY
CHASING TRENDS,
WE'RE ALWAYS
BEHIND.

VINCE PARKER

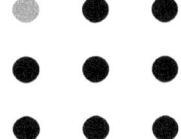

CHAPTER 1

PIONEERING THE FUTURE

In the summer of 1941, a young man named Ted Williams was attempting the impossible, not in a laboratory or on a battlefield, but on a manicured patch of grass, armed with nothing but a wooden stick. Williams was a baseball player, and his goal was to finish the season with a batting average of .400.[1] To the uninitiated, this number may seem arbitrary, but in the world of baseball, it's a hallowed, almost mythical figure. It meant succeeding in four out of every ten attempts to hit the ball—a feat so difficult that no one had accomplished it in over a decade. It was a performance benchmark that separated the excellent from the eternal.

The season was long and grueling, spanning April to October. For months, Williams had held steady, a paragon of consistency. But as the season neared its end, the pressure mounted. On the final day, a doubleheader against the Philadelphia Athletics, his average had dipped to .3995. In baseball, an average is rounded up or down. A final average of .3995 would be rounded up to .400, securing his place in history.[1] He could have chosen to sit out the games, preserving his fragile statistical lead and protecting his legacy. The manager offered him the option. He was safe. The record was, for all intents and purposes, his.

But that's not what pioneers do. They don't play it safe. They don't settle for a mathematical technicality. Williams insisted on playing both games. He chose to step into the future, not back away from it.

He didn't just play; he excelled. In the two games, Williams went six-for-eight, hitting the ball six times out of eight attempts. His final average soared to .406, a number that has never been reached again in the eighty-plus years since.

Williams famously claimed his secret was simple: "I just try to hit the ball where it ain't." He was a student of the game, a meticulous observer who understood not just the physics of the pitch, but the psychology of the pitcher. He didn't just swing at the ball he saw; he swung at the ball he knew was coming. He could anticipate the subtle shifts in a pitcher's grip, the minute changes in arm angle, and the countless small cues that signaled the future. Williams wasn't just reacting to the present; he was playing in the future. He was, in a sense, hitting the ball he couldn't see.

The song "Pioneer" by Cory Asbury aptly captures that it's time to break free from the "treadmill" and the "picket fence of faith."[2] The Church cannot afford to remain stagnant in a world that is constantly evolving. It's time for a generation to overcome the comfort of the familiar or established and emerge as pioneers, venturing into the unknown with a childlike wonder and a willingness to embrace new possibilities. The world is changing, and some would argue that the Church is losing ground at an unprecedented rate, leaving an entire generation behind as it basks in the momentum and resources of a time gone by.

Fair warning, this book will challenge you to move beyond your comfort zone and embrace a new paradigm of mission. It's time to leave behind the old ways and embark on a journey of discovery.

History is littered with explorers who, like the pioneers of faith, dared to venture into the unknown. With his unwavering belief in a new world, Christopher Columbus defied naysayers and sailed into the vast expanse of the Atlantic, forever altering the course of history. The Moroccan scholar Ibn Battuta embarked on extensive journeys across Afro-Eurasia, meticulously documenting his experiences and enriching our understanding of diverse cultures. The Chinese admiral Zheng led impressive voyages, fostering diplomatic ties and expanding trade networks across vast stretches of the Indian Ocean. Amelia Earhart, with her daring spirit, soared to new heights in aviation, pushing the boundaries of what was thought possible.

WILLIAMS WASN'T JUST REACTING TO THE *PRESENT;* HE WAS PLAYING IN THE *FUTURE.*

Rosa Parks, with her quiet courage, ignited a movement for civil rights, challenging the status quo and paving the way for a more just society. Nelson Mandela, who led the fight against apartheid and pioneered a new, democratic South Africa, embodies the transformative power of visionary leadership and unwavering conviction, ushering in a new rainbow nation. Florence Nightingale, with her dedication and innovation, transformed the field of nursing and revolutionized healthcare practices. These pioneers, like many others, embody the spirit of exploration (leaving the known) and innovation (trying alternative methods), both essential for the Church as it navigates the uncharted waters of the 21st century. Their courage, resilience, and unwavering commitment serve as a challenge to those who seek to pioneer new paths and shape a brighter future for the Church.

This book serves as an invitation into what is next and a compass to guide those passionate about Jesus-following as they live and lead, facing the unprecedented challenges of our time. It introduces the concept of "relevance deficit" and equips you with the tools to bridge the gap between the Church and a rapidly changing world. It ushers in conversations about how to adapt to the rapid pace of technological advancements in order to remain relevant.

Together, we explore things like the evolving definition of what it means to be human in the context of technological and societal advancements. Discussing how artificial intelligence, biotechnology, and social movements challenge traditional notions of human identity and value. How do we retain authenticity and build relationships in the digital age? How do we leverage technology to enhance human connection? How do we build a life-giving community in the light of the hyper-individualization of society, creating a post-community society? What is the future of leadership in this new context, and how can we lead with clarity amidst increasing uncertainty?

This book is not a monologue of definitive answers but rather an invitation to join an ongoing, global conversation. It emerges from countless dialogues, distilled from years of wrestling with the same questions that keep you up at night. Instead of presenting polished conclusions, it echoes the reality that an insightful conversation is evolving—exploratory in nature and seeking to articulate the partially formed thoughts you may have already noticed stirring within you.

Think of it as a global gathering of fellow pioneers; you'll encounter stories of others who have stumbled upon insights and wrestled with similar dilemmas. It's an invitation to listen, to learn, and to add your own voice to the chorus. This book doesn't claim to have all the answers; instead, it invites you to become a co-creator in shaping the future of the Church.

The shifts and skills presented in this book have been identified through extensive conversations and actual gatherings of global Christian leaders. In 2022, we facilitated the Not on Our Watch (NOW) conversations, bringing together leaders from every region of the world to share insights on how to address the negative trajectory of Christianity and accelerate the gospel's advancement globally. Another project we were a part of is the "State of the Great Commission Report" by the Lausanne Movement, which provides a detailed overview of the current global mission landscape.[2] This report highlights the urgent need for innovation and adaptation in spiritual formation to reach the next generation effectively.[3] We had the privilege of assisting in facilitating conversations around the missional gaps identified in this report, as over 5,000 leaders from more than 200 nations grappled to understand and innovate solutions for addressing these gaps. Further insights were derived from the "Future of the Gospel" conversation that we facilitated with the World Evangelical Alliance (WEA), which brought together diverse voices to explore the challenges and opportunities facing the Church in the 21st century.[4] This conversation emphasized the importance of collaboration and cross-cultural understanding in fulfilling the Great Commission. Finally, the NextGen and Future of Theological Education conversations at ICETE (International Council for Evangelical Theological Education) provided a platform to specifically address the needs and aspirations of the next generation of leaders with more than 700 theology professors, deans, and presidents of formal and informal theological institutions from every corner of the world.[5] This conversation highlighted the importance of cultivating real connections with the next generation, taking the leap toward creating a community, and developing a lab mentality.

There have also been numerous intentional conversations with young, innovative individuals—sometimes having a naively positive outlook on the future—that have helped shape the conversation resulting in this book. It's beneficial to continue these conversations, whether you have lived through most of the past yourself, feel more tied to it than the present, or still don't fully understand it—even if you belong to an older generation. Don't abdicate leadership, abandon experience, or simply capitulate responsibility to the most willing. Instead, team up with and champion those most focused on, and graced for, the future: the young. Boldly navigate what has been entrusted to you to lead into the future, walking hand in hand with those who will lead well beyond your contribution to the timeline. Allow this book to be a conversation starter and a hope catalyst as you embrace your legacy.

These relationships with amazing people, consultations, conferences, research projects, conversations, and insights gained from the NXT Move community of global leaders have shaped the framework for understanding the shifts and skills necessary for the Church to thrive into the future.[6] Whether directly or indirectly, this book contains contributions from people from every region, culture, and theological stream of the Church. Our prayer is that this diversity of perspectives will be as helpful and inspirational to you as it has been to us.

NAVIGATING THE FUTURE

Navigating the future of faith is like sailing a ship across an open sea, as the pioneers of old. We find ourselves constantly exposed to powerful winds—trends, societal shifts, and technological advancements—that drive us forward, often through unpredictable storms and challenges. While we cannot command these forces or fully control the external elements that impact the Church's journey, we are not mere victims of the currents and tides. Crucially, we possess a rudder and sails: our agency, our discernment, and our strategic choices. Understanding the direction and strength of these winds is paramount. It enables us to skillfully trim our sails and adjust our course, harnessing their power to propel us toward our intended destination, rather than being tossed aimlessly. It is through this intentional understanding and skillful application of our available tools that we can transform potential obstacles into momentum, charting a course that, though influenced by external forces, remains firmly within our deliberate and faithful navigation.

THE CONE OF POSSIBILITY

In this book, we explore how to navigate a rapidly changing world and proactively shape the future of faith. The journey begins with understanding how we perceive and approach the future itself. One powerful way to visualize this is through the "Cone of the Future."[7] Imagine a cone extending from "Now" into "Time," representing "Potential"— everything beyond the present moment.

This cone isn't a solid, predictable path; rather, it's a dynamic landscape composed of various layers of possibility:

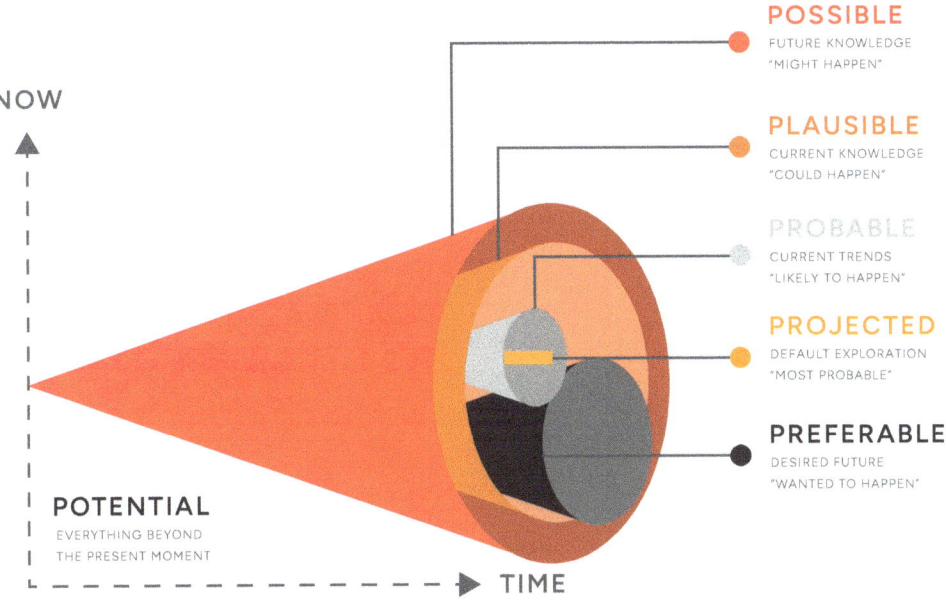

See Hancock, T., & Bezold, C. (1994). Possible futures, preferable futures. The Healthcare Forum Journal, 37(2), 23–29.

• **Possible (Future knowledge - "might happen"):**
This outermost layer encompasses everything that could conceivably happen, limited only by our imagination and the laws of physics. It's the realm of "might happen"— ideas, technologies, or societal shifts currently theoretical or nascent.[7]

• **Plausible (Current knowledge - "could happen"):**
Moving inward, the plausible represents futures that could occur based on our current understanding of the world. These scenarios are logically consistent and within the realm of possibility, even if their likelihood is low.[7]

• **Probable (Current trends - "likely to happen"):**
This layer narrows down the plausible to what is expected to occur if current trends continue unimpeded. It's where we identify patterns and trajectories that suggest a particular future is statistically more probable than others. For example, the increasing

integration of artificial intelligence into daily life is a probable future based on current technological advancements.[7]

• **Projected (Default extrapolation - "most probable"):**
At the very center of the possible, the projected future is the "most probable" outcome if we simply extrapolate from existing data and trends without any intervention or significant shifts. It's the default future we're headed toward if nothing changes, often representing the path of least resistance.[7]

• **Preferable (Desired future - "want to happen"):**
At the core of the cone lies the preferable future—the future we want to happen. This is not a passive prediction, but an active aspiration. It's the desired outcome, the vision we strive to create.[7]

The purpose of leadership is precisely this: to navigate the Cone of the Future, moving beyond simply reacting to the probable or projected and instead intentionally steering toward the preferable.[7]

LEADERSHIP IS

INSIGHT   INFLUENCE   FORESIGHT

Think of leadership as moving people from point A to point B. Point A is where people are— their current understanding, comfort zones, and established ways of doing things. Point B is the preferable future: the foresight, the vision, the desired destination for the Church in an evolving world. The role of leadership, then, is to influence and guide individuals and communities toward that preferred end. If B is the society God dreams about, then it is our role as leaders to steer the world from where they are to this end.

For example, considering the probable future of increasing individualism and a "post-community society," a preferable future for the Church would be one where authentic, life-giving community thrives and is reclaimed as "better." To achieve this, leaders must understand the "Shift to You" phenomenon and proactively foster environments that cultivate connection and belonging.

Similarly, while the digital age presents a probable future of evolving digital existence, the preferable future involves leveraging technology to enhance meaningful relationships and human connection, rather than allowing it to foster isolation.

Understanding this 'Cone of the Future' reveals the landscape in which we must navigate, highlighting the critical shifts that are redefining the context of faith and requiring new skills for effective leadership.

IT WILL TAKE A GOSPEL FREE OF FLUFF

Navigating complexity requires adjusting to shifting currents and winds while maintaining true north. Even as we explore shifts, trends, and skills, we must not lose sight of our true north. The gospel is simple and profound in essence. It appeals to every human being because it meets the heart's deepest needs. God's love, grace, and truth are universal, transcending the complexities of culture and the volatility of changing times. As we strive to reach a world grappling with its own identity, the Church must focus on presenting a gospel free of unnecessary additions.

The goal is not to dilute the message but to strip away the fluff—the layers of tradition, ritual, and systems that sometimes obscure the truth. Like barnacles that grow on ships' hulls and slow them down, so much of what we added to our gospel message has calcified into a message beyond our recognition. Removing these barnacles brings clarity to this timeless message and, in doing so, offers us a gospel that resonates deeply with a generation searching for authenticity and meaning.

This clarity doesn't compromise our faith; it strengthens it. It allows us to confidently declare God's unchanging truths while remaining humble about the mysteries we cannot fully explain. It bridges the gap between the Church and a world desperate for hope, ensuring the beauty and power of the gospel shine brightly in a culture often marked by skepticism and confusion.

Amid the complexity of our digital existence and the rapid acceleration of knowledge, the truth remains constant: authentic love will always be relevant. In fact, the digital age has amplified, not diminished, humanity's longing for connection and life-on-life relationships. This desire, heightened by the isolating effects of digitization, creates a unique opportunity for the Church to meet the emerging generation with clarity, humility, and the fullness of the gospel.

The challenge is significant. If we present the gospel as overly simplistic, overly rational, or a neatly packaged certainty, we risk alienating a generation already overwhelmed by opinions. In a world of noise, we must distinguish between truth and opinion. Truth must be shared as truth, and our opinions as opinions, with humility and authenticity that resonate with a generation seeking clarity.

EMBRACING FAILURE, NOT AS AN END, BUT AS A CATALYST FOR GROWTH, IS AN INDISPENSABLE QUALITY FOR THOSE VENTURING INTO THE FUTURE.

In our quest to present a "gospel free of fluff," we must also ensure we present it with presence. Lisa Pak warns against pushing ahead with our passionate desire for impact without checking if we're still walking with God's rhythm. It's easy to get caught up in streamlining the message, but we must avoid presenting it as an overly simplistic, rushed solution. The core message of God's love and grace must be delivered with authenticity and genuine presence, allowing space for interruptions and the messy realities of life. As Lisa suggests, discerning what not to include can be just as important as what we choose to share—ensuring that the gospel is not just clear but also deeply relational.

Vince Parker, a key next-gen leader from Life.Church, one of the largest and most influential churches in the world, offers a compelling perspective on the future of the Church. He challenges the common temptation to chase cultural trends for relevance, cautioning that "when we're busy chasing trends, we're always behind." Instead, Vince urges the Church to clarify its foundational purpose, asserting, "We don't have to be trendsetters. We stand on the cross—that's enough." While acknowledging the importance of meeting people where they are, online and on social media, he critically questions whether ministries and churches truly align their resources and efforts with their stated mission, emphasizing that in a world of short attention spans, the answer isn't to become trendier, it's remembering the core message of the cross and standing firm in the mission God has called you to.

FAILURE AS A CATALYST FOR GROWTH

True pioneers understand that the path into the unknown is rarely smooth. Just as explorers face storms and unexpected detours, the journey of faith and innovation will inevitably encounter setbacks. Embracing failure, not as an end but as a catalyst for growth, is an indispensable quality for those venturing into the future.

Embracing failure is key as we explore leading into the future. We understand that not everyone finds comfort in failure. Failure is often seen as something to avoid, but it's a necessary part of growth and innovation in our fast-paced world. Projects may not always hit the mark, but these moments should be viewed as valuable detours leading to more significant opportunities. Take Apple's failed circular mouse or Google Glass—both became significant learning moments that propelled these companies toward even better innovations. This mindset is essential for any organization. We need to cultivate an experimental mindset—one that embraces risk, learns from failure, and continues innovating until we discover what truly works.

Thomas Edison famously said, "I haven't failed; I've just discovered 10,000 ways that don't work." Imagine if Thomas Edison had decided to quit after facing initial obstacles with inventing the lightbulb. This perspective turns setbacks into valuable learning opportunities that fuel personal and organizational growth. Whether in ministry, new initiatives, or personal development, failure can ultimately guide us to refine and improve our approach to fulfilling our mission amid future shifts.

In our experiments and initiatives, we need to pause, recalibrate, and discern whether our failures are leading us closer to or further away from our true mission. It's not just about trying new things but also about discerning which detours are Spirit-led and which are simply distractions. This requires a balance of urgency to act and the wisdom to discern God's specific guidance in each situation.

To adapt effectively to the ever-evolving landscape, we need leaders who are prepared for what lies ahead—individuals equipped with a spectrum of skills and diverse perspectives. The first step in this journey is identifying those with sensitivity, an invaluable trait in today's interconnected and multifaceted world. Effective leaders must skillfully navigate diverse cultural environments, like an experienced surfer gracefully riding the waves, demonstrating adaptability and respect for the powerful forces at play.

This book is designed to be your compass and guide. By understanding the "shifts" impacting humanity, digital existence, trust, organizational dynamics, and community, and by developing the "skills" necessary to navigate them, we can intentionally hit the ball we cannot yet clearly see. We can move beyond simply reacting to what's likely and instead actively pioneer and co-create the brighter, preferable future God has in store for the Church. This is an invitation to join a global conversation, to learn, and to contribute your voice to shaping the next season of the Church. You are invited to embrace the pioneer spirit, join the conversation, and discover the new horizons God has in store for us. We believe the future of the Church is bright, for it is ultimately Christ who builds His Church. He is faithful and able to make a way. Raise leaders. Reach generations. This book is a prayer that, in obedience, we might find and fulfill our part in His story for the next season of the Church. Our role is to faithfully follow His leading, seeking His wisdom and guidance as we navigate the challenges and opportunities of our time. By aligning ourselves with His purposes and seeking His Kingdom first, we can trust Him to empower us to fulfill His mission in the world.

As we navigate uncharted waters, let us embrace a pioneering spirit, trusting in God's guidance to illuminate our hearts and reveal the realities surrounding us. Let us not be paralyzed by the fear of failure or the unknown, but emboldened by the knowledge that God is with us every step of the way. He is shaping us—His Church and our organizations—for a future in which we can effectively reach and minister to the hearts of generations to come. May we have the courage to adapt, the wisdom to discern, and the unwavering faith to trust that God will lead us faithfully into the future He has prepared, the future He prefers.

CHAPTER 1 SUMMARY

The book aims to be a compass for leaders by exploring key global shifts and equipping them with the skills to navigate the future of faith. It frames leadership as steering toward a "preferable future" by understanding the present and actively influencing the direction of the Church, rather than just reacting to trends. Drawing from insights gathered from global conversations and research, the chapter sets the stage for a collaborative journey, encouraging leaders to embrace an innovative, pioneering spirit to advance the gospel effectively.

REFLECTIVE QUESTIONS

1. What past momentum or inherited resources are you still relying on that may no longer serve your current context?

2. What is your "preferable future" for the Church or your community, and how are you leading toward it?

3. What shifts are you noticing in your faith community or region that might require pioneering responses?

HOW YOU CAN
JOIN THE CONVERSATION

This book isn't a final word—it's a starting point. A launching pad into the conversations, collaborations, and callings that will shape what comes next.

To carry this conversation forward, we've partnered with the Lausanne Movement and the State of the Great Commission Report to create an online space where shared mission becomes movement.

Here in the Lausanne Action Hub, *Hitting the Ball You Cannot See, Conversations on the Future of Jesus-Following*, you'll find the same shifts and skills explored in the book, but opened up for dialogue.

You'll gain access to exclusive interviews with global leaders and also see some of the original interviews conducted in the process of writing this book. Their voices—raw, wise, faith-filled—will ground these shifts in lived experience and inspire you to step boldly into what's next.

But don't walk this road alone. Each lesson includes a space for you to add your voice—to ask questions, share insights, and learn from others. When we reflect together, we don't just read—we relate. We don't just consume—we collaborate.

TO BEGIN, SCAN THE QR CODE BELOW:

It's as simple as the following:

1. Sign up or Sign in to the Lausanne Action Hub

2. Access the *"Hitting the Ball You Cannot See, Conversations on the Future of Jesus-Following"* space.

3. Start collaborating with like-minded leaders on the future of Jesus-following.

Powered by the

MAYBE *FAITHFULNESS*
IS LEARNING TO
SWING WHERE THE
BALL *WILL BE.*

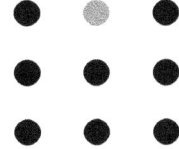

CHAPTER 2

HITTING THE BALL YOU CANNOT SEE

FASTER THAN THE EYE CAN SEE

We see the impossible happen almost every single weekend. Large crowds gather in colosseum-esque theaters of triumph and disaster to see the edge of human possibility exceeded in moments of brilliance. In sporting arenas from Mumbai to Cape Town, to a borough of Queens in New York City, the impossible has been conquered. Countless home runs, returns of serve, and reverse-sweep sixes remind us that the impossible has become the anticipated, and the exception is now the norm. Take Major League Baseball (MLB), for example, where fastballs routinely average at least 90 miles per hour, or 144 kilometers per hour.[1] The sheer velocity of MLB fastballs translates into incredibly short timeframes for the athlete facing them. A fastballs pitched at 90 miles per hour reaches the home plate in 425 milliseconds or 0.425 seconds.[1] To put this into perspective, a human eye blink takes about 300 to 400 ms, meaning the ball literally arrives in the blink of an eye.[1]

It takes about 200 ms to perceive and recognize the ball coming at you.[1] People differ, but it takes roughly 275 ms for the signal to travel from your eye to your brain and down to your hand—and another 150 ms to swing the bat.[1]

From the moment the ball leaves the pitcher's hand to the point of contact with the bat, only 458 milliseconds pass. For the batter, however, it takes roughly 200 milliseconds to visually process the pitch, 275 milliseconds for the brain to send the signal to the muscles, and another 150 milliseconds to complete the swing—totaling 625 milliseconds. That's 167 milliseconds too late. Biologically and physically impossible—yet, every week, thousands of these 'impossible' hits are made.

Returning a 90 mile per hour pitch is less about possessing superhuman reflexes and more about developing advanced anticipatory capabilities, acting preemptively, and making adjustments on the way. Simply stated, it is less about our ability to react and more about our ability to anticipate. It is not about seeing the ball faster, but about seeing and responding to the ball smarter. This is what hitting the ball we cannot see is all about. This is what leading into the future requires of us.

THE FASTBALL WE ARE FACING

We are living in a time of unprecedented acceleration. Human progress between 2025 and 1925 far surpasses the advancements between 1925 and 925, with the past century transforming our world more than the preceding millennium. This is reflected in the astonishing pace of knowledge growth.[2] In 1900, collective knowledge doubled every 100 years; by 1942, every 25 years; by 1982, every 13 months; and today, it is believed to double every 12 hours.[3] If you have been struggling to keep up with the rate of technological development or new words Gen Alpha is coming up with, you know what I am talking about. The world has constantly been changing, and humanity has not had this rate of exponential change to contend with at any point in our existence. As believers, we are often trying to hit the ball where it is, or even was, but maybe faithfulness is learning to swing where the ball will be.

Every individual and organization has a relevance quotient (or level of relevance)—a measure of how effectively they remain connected and meaningful in a rapidly changing world. When the pace of change outside an individual or organization exceeds the pace of change within, its level of relevance begins to decline. Its methods are no longer optimal for impact or embrace. It has become irrelevant. Much of the global Church is struggling to keep up with the rate of change people are experiencing. When the global Church struggles to keep up, we operate with a relevance deficit.

Martec's Law highlights this challenge, emphasizing that irrelevance follows when external change outpaces internal adaptation.[4]

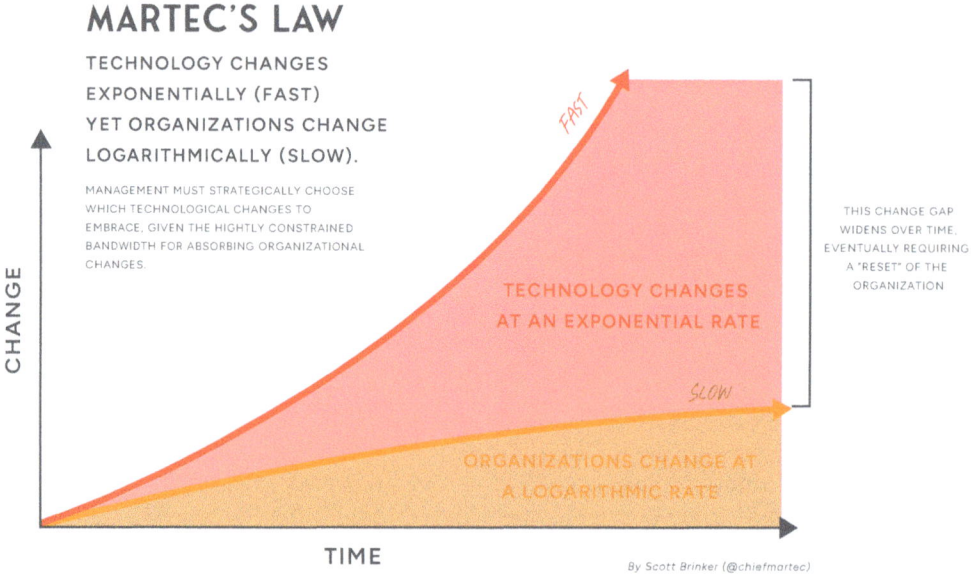

MARTEC'S LAW

TECHNOLOGY CHANGES EXPONENTIALLY (FAST) YET ORGANIZATIONS CHANGE LOGARITHMICALLY (SLOW).

MANAGEMENT MUST STRATEGICALLY CHOOSE WHICH TECHNOLOGICAL CHANGES TO EMBRACE, GIVEN THE HIGHTLY CONSTRAINED BANDWIDTH FOR ABSORBING ORGANIZATIONAL CHANGES.

CHANGE

FAST

TECHNOLOGY CHANGES AT AN EXPONENTIAL RATE

SLOW

THIS CHANGE GAP WIDENS OVER TIME, EVENTUALLY REQUIRING A "RESET" OF THE ORGANIZATION

ORGANIZATIONS CHANGE AT A LOGARITHMIC RATE

TIME

By Scott Brinker (@chiefmartec)

To understand the potential for irrelevance, consider the rapid evolution of communication. For centuries, physical letters reigned supreme, connecting people across vast distances. Then came the telephone, offering instant conversations but tethered to a location. Mobile phones liberated us from those tethers, and with each iteration, from clunky devices to sleek smartphones, the pace of change accelerated. Text messaging evolved from multi-tap to predictive text to full keyboards, eventually giving way to the intuitive touchscreens and voice typing we use today. This constant evolution, driven by technological advancements at an ever-increasing rate, has shrunk the lifespan of dominant communication methods. Consider the fact that for more than 100 years, from its invention in 1876 to the early 2000s, the landline phone was a prevalent form of communication.[4] What once took decades or centuries to become obsolete now happens in a few short years, even months.

IT IS LESS ABOUT OUR ABILITY TO *REACT* AND MORE ABOUT OUR ABILITY TO *ANTICIPATE.*

This accelerating pace of change presents a critical challenge for any institution, including faith communities. We risk becoming irrelevant if we cling to outdated methods and fail to adapt to the evolving ways people connect and communicate. Just as the telegraph gave way to the telephone and the landline to the mobile phone, faith communities must also embrace new technologies and platforms to remain relevant in a rapidly changing world.

This requires not just adopting new tools, but also understanding the underlying shifts in how people consume information, form communities, and seek meaning in their lives. Failing to do so could lead to a gradual decline in engagement and influence, particularly as younger generations turn to more dynamic and accessible sources of connection and inspiration.

A loss of relevance results in a loss of connection. If our mission is to reach the world, how do we do that if we become disconnected from it? Much of the Church is operating at a relevance deficit, not due to an outdated gospel or irrelevant mission, but because it has gotten stuck in irrelevant methodologies.

In Carey Nieuwhof's insightful exploration of relevance, he challenges us to put mission above method.[5] This means adapting our methods to remain relevant, rather than altering the mission itself. The Church's mission—the gospel's message—remains as potent as ever, but the methods we employ to deliver that message must adapt to the ever-changing landscape. Our strategies and approaches shouldn't be held as sacred; they are simply tools to achieve a higher purpose. By prioritizing the unchanging mission over potentially outdated methods, we open ourselves up to innovation, flexibility, and a greater capacity to connect with a world in constant flux. Nieuwhof's words resonate deeply with the call for a "gospel free of fluff," urging us to shed unnecessary additions and present the core message with clarity and authenticity.[5] In a rapidly evolving world, clinging to rigid methodologies hinders our ability to engage and serve genuinely. Unless we remain adaptable, willing to evolve our approach while keeping our eyes fixed on the ultimate goal, the gospel may be seen as irrelevant, when in reality, it's the methods that are outdated. People do not necessarily distinguish the gospel from the method.

Unfortunately, it would appear that in some parts of the global church, we are not doing this well. In the USA, there is a visible decline in church retention and evangelism rates. Projections suggest that by 2050, 42 million young people could leave the Church—a trend termed "The Great Dechurching."[6] Though we are noticing islands of revival in a sea of decline, and some recent studies have even suggested a resurgence of faith in some generations, others argue it's merely a statistical anomaly, with the broader decline continuing to deepen.

The gospel's message remains powerful, but translating it effectively for a new generation requires intentional, adaptive strategies. By learning from the past and embracing present opportunities, the Church can ensure its enduring relevance and impact in a rapidly changing world.

Lisa Pak, a second-generation Korean-Canadian and Toronto native, serves as the Director of Partnerships (Asia) at Finishing The Task. With a focus on collaborative efforts to empower women and rising generations for Kingdom purpose, she brings a uniquely insightful perspective to every conversation—offering wisdom that speaks directly to our desire to bridge the relevance deficit. She says, "Jesus was urgent, yes, but never rushed." It's tempting to rush into adopting every new trend or technology. We must be careful not to prioritize speed over substance, or activity over presence. True relevance isn't just about keeping up with the world's pace; it's about being in step with the Spirit. This means taking time to discern which methods truly align with our mission and which are simply fleeting distractions. We need to marry our urgency to reach the world with discernment, ensuring that our strategies are not just timely but also deeply rooted in God's rhythm.

> JESUS WAS
>
> *URGENT*, YES,
>
> BUT NEVER *RUSHED*.
>
> **LISA PAK**

UNDERSTANDING CHANGE

If change is the process through which the future invades our lives, then change is an ever-present reality that impacts individuals and organizations, demanding adaptability and a willingness to evolve. To navigate this dynamic landscape effectively, it's crucial to understand the catalysts that drive change and how we can respond constructively.

Change is a constant. As the future unfolds, it inevitably "invades our lives," impacting us in various ways. Understanding how change happens is crucial to navigating it effectively. Let's explore the four catalysts that bring about change: crisis, disruption, innovation, and obedience.

THE 4 CHANGE CATALYSTS

1.**Crisis:** This is an unexpected, external event that disrupts life. A crisis demands immediate adaptation and can drastically alter the course of events. The Second World War and the global pandemic are prime examples of crises that have caused widespread change. In the case of the pandemic, it also accelerated changes already underway, such as the rise of video conferencing and remote work.

2. **Disruption:** Unlike a crisis, disruption is a gradual process. It's an external shift that challenges existing norms, requiring flexibility and new approaches. While it may not be as sudden as a crisis, disruption can still lead to significant change over time.

WHEN THE *RATE OF CHANGE* OUTSIDE AN INDIVIDUAL OR ORGANIZATION EXCEEDS THE RATE OF CHANGE INSIDE THAT ENTITY, ITS LEVEL OF *RELEVANCE BECOMES DEFICIENT.*

3. **Innovation:** This catalyst is typically positive and involves self-initiated action. Innovation leads to personal or collective growth and improvement. It's the problem-solving and creative thinking that occurs over time to improve things.

4. **Obedience:** It might seem surprising, but obedience can be a powerful catalyst for change. Acts of obedience—like Martin Luther's 95 Theses or John Wesley's missionary journeys—have profoundly shaped the course of history.

Crisis, disruption, innovation, and obedience are each catalysts that play a distinct role in influencing the trajectory of our world.

UNDERSTANDING CHANGE QUADRANTS

To better understand change, it's helpful to consider it within a quadrants framework. This framework involves two axes: unchanging/changing and known/unknown.

- **Unchanging and Changing:** In any situation, some elements remain constant, while others are subject to change. It's important to recognize both in order to respond appropriately.

- **Knowns and Unknowns:** Some changes are immediately apparent, while others may surprise us. Similarly, some unchanging elements may be obvious, while others remain unknown.

The Change Quadrants help us categorize our awareness and understanding of change, allowing for more effective responses .

CHANGE QUADRANTS

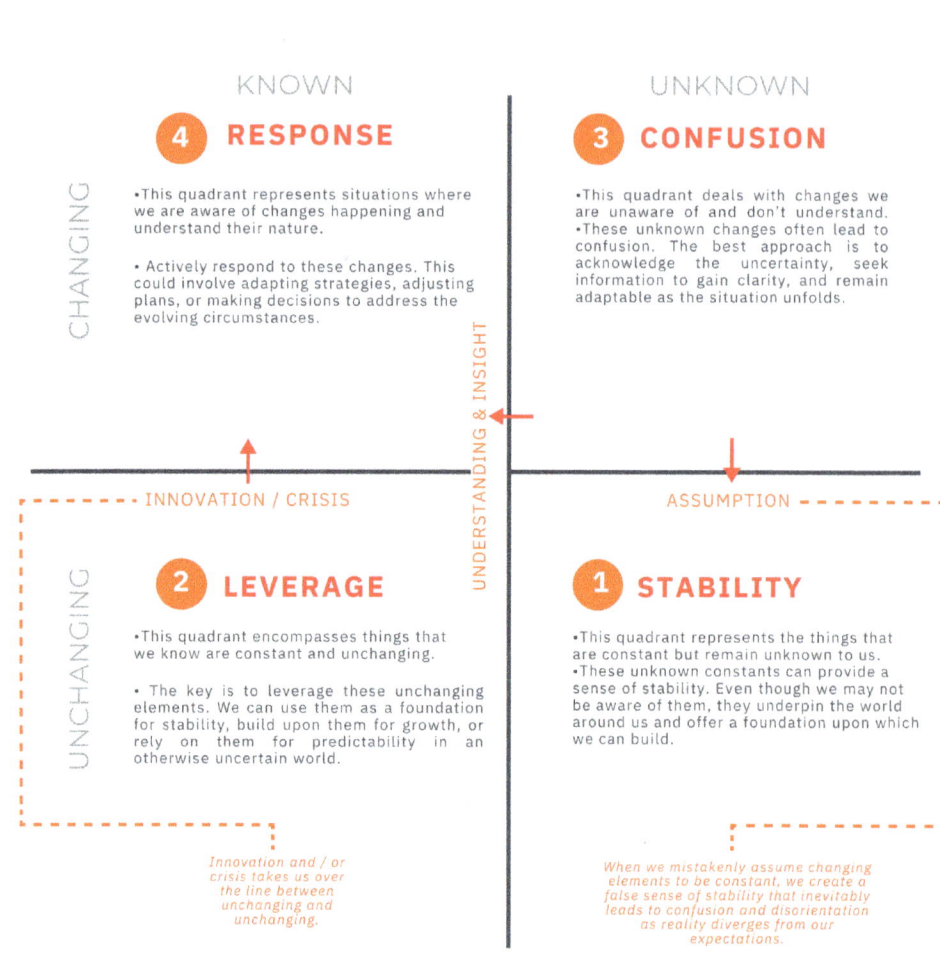

KNOWN

UNKNOWN

4 RESPONSE

3 CONFUSION

CHANGING

- •This quadrant represents situations where we are aware of changes happening and understand their nature.

- • Actively respond to these changes. This could involve adapting strategies, adjusting plans, or making decisions to address the evolving circumstances.

- •This quadrant deals with changes we are unaware of and don't understand.
- •These unknown changes often lead to confusion. The best approach is to acknowledge the uncertainty, seek information to gain clarity, and remain adaptable as the situation unfolds.

UNDERSTANDING & INSIGHT

INNOVATION / CRISIS

ASSUMPTION

2 LEVERAGE

1 STABILITY

UNCHANGING

- •This quadrant encompasses things that we know are constant and unchanging.

- • The key is to leverage these unchanging elements. We can use them as a foundation for stability, build upon them for growth, or rely on them for predictability in an otherwise uncertain world.

- •This quadrant represents the things that are constant but remain unknown to us.
- •These unknown constants can provide a sense of stability. Even though we may not be aware of them, they underpin the world around us and offer a foundation upon which we can build.

Innovation and / or crisis takes us over the line between unchanging and unchanging.

When we mistakenly assume changing elements to be constant, we create a false sense of stability that inevitably leads to confusion and disorientation as reality diverges from our expectations.

By recognizing these different quadrants, we can tailor our responses to navigate change more effectively. Whether it's responding to known shifts, leveraging unchanging elements, seeking clarity amidst confusion, or finding solace in hidden stability, each quadrant presents a unique opportunity for growth and adaptation.

Quadrant 1: Stability (Unknown/Unchanging) represents elements that remain constant but are unknown to us. These unknown constants can provide a sense of stability and serve as a foundation, even if we are unaware of them. For example, the love and grace of God might be unknown to some, but they are still an unchanging element holding the world together. One doesn't have to understand gravity in order to be held in place by it. However, mistakenly assuming that changing elements, such as government or other human institutions, are constant can create a false sense of stability, leading to confusion when reality diverges from these expectations.

Quadrant 2: Leverage (Known/Unchanging) focuses on elements we recognize as constant and unchanging. To truly utilize stability, we must identify these unchanging elements, such as the magnificence of the love of God, and move them from the unknown to the known. By acknowledging these constants, we can leverage them as a foundation for stability, build upon them for growth, and rely on them for predictability in an uncertain world. God is always good, whether one knows it or not, but His goodness only becomes a source of hope when it is recognized and received. Just like the aerodynamic principles that have always governed flight: they were constant all along, but only became useful once they were understood.

Quadrant 3: Confusion (Unknown/Changing) describes situations where changes are occurring but are unknown to us, leading to organizational struggles due to not adapting quickly enough. This quadrant addresses changes we are unaware of and don't understand, often resulting in confusion and ultimately irrelevance. The best approach is to acknowledge the uncertainty, actively seek information to gain clarity, and remain adaptable as the situation unfolds. Very few things need to remain in this quadrant, with most changes becoming known over time.

Quadrant 4: Response (Known/Changing) involves situations where we are aware of changes and understand their nature. By identifying and understanding these changes, we can move from confusion to response, making the unknown known and allowing us to adapt and take action. This quadrant requires us to actively respond to these changes, which could involve adapting strategies, adjusting plans, or making decisions to address the evolving circumstances.

IDENTIFYING AND RESPONDING TO KEY SHIFTS

In the realm of navigation, there exists a technique called dead reckoning—a method employed to estimate one's current position based on a previously determined location and an estimate of the subsequent movements. In the same way we must identify key trends and their possible implications in order to try to anticipate a possible future. Similarly, when receiving a call from someone who is lost, our first step is to ask about their current location. We can only lead people to a destination, if we first understand where they are.

True leadership requires a clear grasp of both the current reality and the individuals you're guiding. Without this, leadership becomes akin to embarking on a journey without a map or trying to solve a problem without knowing its root cause.

As we identify and respond to key shifts, we must keep in mind Lisa's reminder: "Understanding the times doesn't mean we have to move at the world's pace." While being aware of cultural and technological changes is essential, our response should be guided by spiritual discernment, not just a reaction to external pressures. We need to be like sailors, adjusting to shifting currents and winds, yet always keeping our eyes fixed on our "true north." This means pausing to recalibrate, discerning God's specific calling in each situation, and ensuring that our strategies are in step with the Spirit's rhythm.

Speed doesn't always mean significance. The kingdom isn't hurried. It's rooted.

The essence of leadership lies in the ability to inspire and guide individuals toward a shared objective. However, this ability is intrinsically linked to the leader's grasp of the current situation and the specific needs of those they lead. Just as a ship's captain must be cognizant of their vessel's current coordinates before charting a course—and just as we must locate a lost caller before giving directions—a leader must first understand the present moment. Growing in awareness of the shifts and trends shaping this season is essential to leading with clarity and purpose.

Jenn Brown, a key leader in one of the most innovative and influential Bible engagement strategies for the next generation, OneHope, emphasizes that the urgency of the future is not just about responding to what is, it's about learning to anticipate what might be. Drawing from their own research and leadership within global missional networks, Jenn doesn't just reflect on trends, she presses hard into the unseen horizon. Peter Drucker, the leadership coach, said: "The greatest danger in times of turbulence is not the turbulence itself, but to act with yesterday's logic."[7]

HITTING A HOME RUN

We don't just need faster reflexes—we need sharper foresight. The leaders of tomorrow must be flexible enough to respond to changing circumstances while remaining authentic to their values and principles. The faster the fastballs are coming at us, the more the curveballs are shifting through the air, the better we need to become at anticipating the trajectory, and the greater skill we need to have at adapting our swing to hit the ball.

This isn't just about making contact; it's about swinging for the fences, aiming for the kind of impact that changes the game. The fastball we're facing, this era of unprecedented acceleration and shifting realities, is indeed faster than the eye can see. It demands more than just a reaction; it calls for anticipation, for smart, preemptive action. And in the grand stadium of faith, what we're doing—seeking to accelerate Christianity into the future as we navigate complex shifts and build a thriving Church for generations to come—is simply too dear, too important, and too valuable to miss this ball.

CHAPTER 2 SUMMARY

This chapter uses the analogy of a baseball player hitting a fastball to illustrate the need for anticipation rather than reaction in Christian leadership. It highlights the unprecedented speed of change in modern society, where knowledge doubles every 12 hours. This rapid change creates a "relevance deficit" for the church when its internal rate of change fails to keep pace. The chapter introduces the concept of Martec's Law. It explores four catalysts for change—crisis, disruption, innovation, and obedience—as well as the "Change Quadrants" framework (Stability, Leverage, Confusion, Respond) to help leaders understand and navigate these shifts. It emphasizes that faithfulness in this era means learning to swing where the ball will be, not where it is, by prioritizing the unchanging mission over outdated methods.

REFLECTIVE QUESTIONS

1. Where in your leadership or ministry are you trying to "hit the ball where it used to be" rather than where it's going?

2. What spiritual practices help you anticipate rather than simply react?

3. What "true north" helps you recalibrate when trends feel disorienting?

JOIN THE CONVERSATION
& WATCH THE INTERVIEWS HERE

SPEED DOESN'T
ALWAYS MEAN
SIGNIFICANCE.
THE KINGDOM
ISN'T HURRIED–
IT'S ROOTED.

INTRODUCTION

TO THE SHIFTS & SKILLS FOR THE FUTURE OF FAITH

You are living in a time of unprecedented acceleration, with human progress in the last century far surpassing that of the preceding millennium. This rapid pace, often referred to as a fastball, demands a new kind of leadership. Just as a baseball player anticipates the ball's trajectory to make contact, we must learn to swing where the ball will be. The global Church is currently struggling with a relevance deficit because the pace of change outside the institution is exceeding the pace of change within. Our mission—the gospel—remains unchanging, but our methods must adapt to the world around us.

To overcome this, we must first understand the ground on which we stand. The following chapters will identify six key shifts that are reshaping our world, and we will explore these shifts through three distinct ways our world is changing: how we live, how the world works, and how we connect. This framework helps us recognize that the challenges we face are not isolated, but interconnected facets of a new reality.

PART 1: HOW WE LIVE (EXPERIENTIAL)

The first two shifts address the fundamental, internal crisis of human existence. In a world of dizzying technological and social change, the very definition of who we are is being redefined.

- **Shifting Definition of Being Human (Chapter 3):** The core concept of what it means to be human is changing, as advancements in artificial intelligence and biotechnology blur the lines between creation and creator.

- **Shifting Delineations of Digital Existence (Chapter 4):** Our digital lives are no longer just tools—they've become a defining aspect of our reality, reshaping how we communicate, form our identities, and even perceive truth.

These shifts create a fraught foundation—where traditional anchors of identity and reality are fraying, leaving many with a deep sense of internal disorientation.

PART 2: HOW THE WORLD WORKS (STRUCTURAL)

The next pair of shifts examines the external, systemic consequences of this personal unraveling. When individuals lose their sense of certainty, trust in the institutions that once offered stability begins to erode.

- **Shifting Dynamics of Trust (Chapter 5):** The societal bell curve of shared reality has given way to an inverse bell curve of polarization, where the middle ground has collapsed and mistrust in institutions is rampant.

- **Shifting Dimensions of Organization (Chapter 6):** This breakdown of trust, combined with the accelerating pace of technology, is causing old organizational structures to deteriorate. This is forcing a re-evaluation of how companies, governments, and even the church are structured and led.

Together, these shifts represent a context revolution where the external world of work, politics, and media is becoming more fragmented and difficult to navigate.

PART 3: HOW WE CONNECT (RELATIONAL)

The final two shifts focus on the most profound challenge and opportunity for the church: our relational existence. In a world of frayed foundations and unraveling institutions, the need for genuine connection has never been greater.

• **Shifting Degrees of Separation (Chapter 7):** Despite technology collapsing the distance between people, a new *Paradox of Proximity* has emerged, where we are more connected than ever, yet increasingly isolated and lonely.

• **Shifting Discovery of Belonging (Chapter 8):** This paradox has given rise to a post-community society, where people search for belonging in new ways, often online or through shared interests, rather than through traditional communities.

These shifts represent a connection rewiring, a fundamental change in how we relate to one another. The Church's task is to not only understand this rewiring but to become the path to true, authentic reconnection, moving beyond passive observation to active, committed participation. By understanding these three areas of change—the experiential, the structural, and the relational—we can begin to develop the skills necessary to hit the ball we cannot yet see.

How the world is changing?

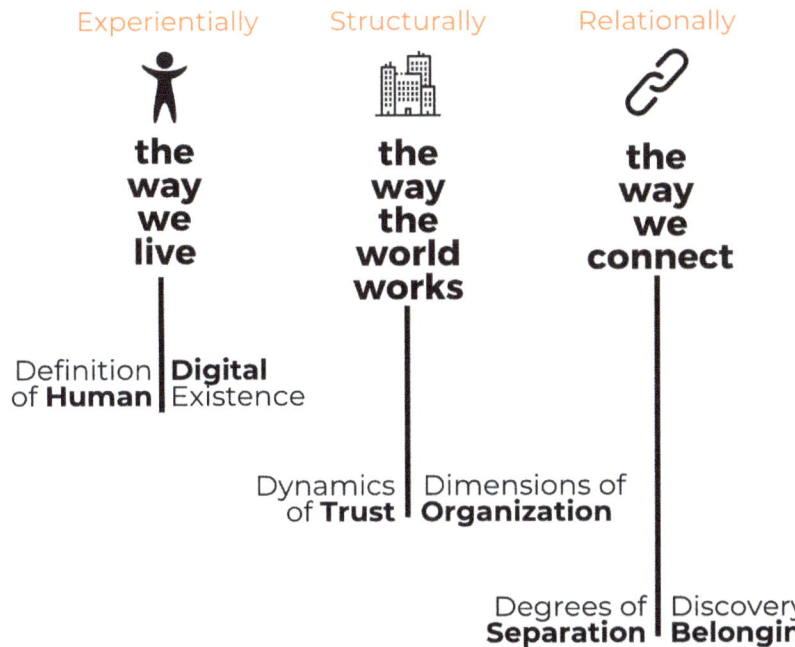

Experientially · Structurally · Relationally

the way we live · the way the world works · the way we connect

Definition of **Human** | **Digital** Existence

Dynamics of **Trust** | Dimensions of **Organization**

Degrees of **Separation** | Discovery of **Belonging**

IF YOU ARE THE TYPE OF PERSON THAT READS THE LAST PAGE OF THE BOOK FIRST OR IF YOU NEED THINGS IN NEAT BOXES, YOU MIGHT WANT TO HAVE A LOOK AT THE TABLE ON **PAGE 147** BEFORE JUMPING INTO THE DETAILS OF THE SHIFTS AND SKILLS.

PART 1

HOW WE LIVE
(EXPERIENTIAL)

BUT THERE IS *HOPE*.
THERE IS A VOICE
OF TRUTH THAT
STILL SPEAKS.
THERE IS A JESUS
WHO RESTORES.
AND THERE IS
A GENERATION –
WOUNDED BUT
SEARCHING –
THAT IS STILL
LONGING FOR
PURPOSE.

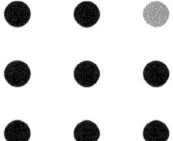

CHAPTER 3

SHIFTING DEFINITION OF BEING HUMAN

In a world of dizzying technological and social change, the very definition of who we are is being redefined. This fundamental shift lies at the core of how we experience our human existence, leaving many with a deep sense of disorientation. On an ordinary June day in Northern California, four seemingly unrelated events unfolded within an hour's drive of each other. These moments, unnoticed by many, reflected a more profound cultural transformation quietly reshaping how we view human identity and our collective future.

In 2007, Steve Jobs introduced the iPhone, revolutionizing communication and connectivity.[1] Fast forward to 2024, when Jensen Huang, CEO of NVIDIA, unveiled the Blackwell GPU platform.[2] Unlike tools that extend human capabilities, this innovation blurred the boundaries between human and machine. As real-time AI applications became reality, deep questions emerged: Can machines replicate creativity and intelligence? And if they can, what truly defines humanity, and what remains irreplaceable?

Meanwhile, in San Jose, a Pride flag was raised in a ceremony at City Hall hosted by the Family and Children's Services of Silicon Valley. LGBTQ youth and their allies celebrated this Inclusion Act, symbolizing progress and the ongoing fight for recognition.[3] Community leaders took to the podium, celebrating diversity and denouncing hate. The Pride flag, flying alongside the U.S. flag, stood as a testament to the evolving ways identity is expressed and valued today.

Nearby, Dr. Jennifer Doudna's team advanced CRISPR technology at Berkeley's Innovative Genomics Institute, offering humanity the power to alter genetic code.[4] From curing genetic disorders to improving food security, this innovation pushes the boundaries of biology and raises questions about humanity's role in shaping its own future. The team worked to refine gene editing and delivery methods, tackling profound issues while redefining human potential.

At Stanford's Hasso Plattner Institute of Design, researchers explored identity through the lens of intersectionality. They created a $35 deck of cards to help designers consider individuals' complex, multifaceted experiences, such as gender, ethnicity, and orientation.[5] Each card offered insights into the subjective lives of others, urging creators to design with inclusivity and empathy, transforming the relationship between humanity and innovation.

Within an hour's drive in northern California, over a span of seventeen years, four parallel stories occurred, ranging from technological breakthroughs to social advocacy, from scientific research to creative empathy. These stories, a stone's throw away from each other, prompt the same question that has been asked throughout human history: What does it mean to be human?

SHIFTS:

A SHIFTING DEFINITION

In ancient Greece and Rome, the first significant concept of humanity emerged: we are rational beings. This understanding laid the groundwork for defining humanity by our ability to think, reason, and make sense of the world. The Renaissance elevated the human body as a symbol of beauty and perfection. The statues of that period, from Greece to Paris, glorified humanity as the crown of creation. Human gods were depicted in our form, celebrating humanity itself as the ultimate object of admiration and worship. Later, the Enlightenment and the scientific revolution took the focus further, emphasizing the power of understanding. Thinkers like Darwin and Freud explored evolutionary theory, consciousness, and identity, adding complexity to what defines our existence.

From these foundations, humanity's definition continued to evolve, shaped by neuroscience, cognitive science, and more recently, posthumanism and transhumanism. These fields are raising questions previously confined to science fiction—such as: If we can create human life without sperm or eggs, is it a human being? If technology allows us to augment our physical forms or transfer consciousness to a digital platform, what remains of the essence of humanity? These advances force us to wrestle with profound ethical and existential dilemmas.

Technological advances—particularly artificial intelligence (AI) and biotechnology—reshape how society views identity, value, and existence. In the State of the Great Commission report, it is observed that while the church is currently focused on addressing issues related to the sexual revolution and identity, the next major challenge will likely center on the very essence of humanity.[6]

What defines a human being? What gives a person value as a human? These questions are becoming increasingly relevant as society grapples with concepts like transhumanism,[7] generative AI,[8] and biotech advancements that challenge the boundaries of human identity. Artificial intelligence is rapidly evolving, with language models and generative AI now producing human-like content—and even writing code autonomously. Remarkably, much of today's AI advancements are being driven by other AI systems themselves—AI creating AI.[9] This raises important ethical and societal questions about machines that learn and innovate beyond human understanding. Concurrently, biotechnology breakthroughs in anti-aging, physical augmentation, and consciousness transfer push the boundaries of transhumanism,[7] prompting us to rethink human identity in a digital or biologically enhanced future. Ultimately, these advancements challenge us to define what it truly means to be human.

Steiger Europe's Ania Greenwood has spent years working with young people across Europe and beyond. From Poland to Brazil to the UK, for her, one theme continues to rise to the surface: "Identity is no longer just a struggle—it's a full-blown crisis. In earlier generations, young people would ask questions like, 'Who am I?' or 'What is my purpose?'"

But today, Ania observes a more haunting question: "'Why am I like this?' The shift is subtle but significant. It's not just about finding direction anymore—it's about questioning existence. This internal disorientation is resulting in rising levels of mental illness, anxiety, depression, and self-harm."

Humanity's self-definition has shifted across eras, each adding a new perspective:

1. **"I survive; therefore, I am."** In ancient times, survival defined humanity. Being at the top of the food chain validated our existence.

2. **"I make, therefore I am."** The ability to create—fire, wheels, tools—ushered in an era where value was tied to innovation. Human identity became rooted in what we could produce and accomplish.

3. **"I think, therefore I am."** The Age of Reason elevated thought and consciousness as uniquely human traits. Our intellectual capacities became central to our sense of self.

4. **"I feel, therefore I am."** The emotional revolution followed, highlighting feelings as essential to humanity. Emotions, vulnerability, and even tears began to be seen not as weaknesses, but as markers of authenticity and connection.

5. **"I create; therefore, I am."** Today's influencer-driven culture elevates creativity as the pinnacle of human identity. Figures like Taylor Swift, celebrated for their creative contributions, exemplify how society now defines value through artistic expression.

The challenge? Each of these functions—surviving, creating, thinking, and feeling—can now be replicated by artificial intelligence. Machines can perform tasks once considered uniquely human. They can make art, write music, analyze data, and even simulate emotions. If AI can do these things, does that diminish what it means to be human? Amid all this, Ania notes that the future feels fragile. The rise of technology, combined with a generation's deep insecurities, is fueling a surge of existential questions: "What is my purpose if machines can do it all?"

THE DEEPER QUESTION

At first glance, these stories—spanning science, technology, and social movements—appear vastly different, yet they all wrestle with the same profound theme: *What does it mean to be human?*

AI breakthroughs have sparked a conversation that challenges our understanding of human uniqueness. Unlike past technologies, AI now performs tasks once believed to be exclusively human, surpassing human capacity in writing, speech recognition, and even complex decision-making. These developments force us to confront a new question: Can machines think and act like humans? What defining attributes set humans apart from the artificial constructs we create? As AI advances, it raises profound questions about human uniqueness, autonomy, and what truly sets us apart in a world where machines may one day replicate, rival, or surpass our cognitive abilities.

Similarly, the rise of LGBTQ identity and evolving sexual ideologies has sparked a philosophical revolution regarding identity. These movements challenge long-held views about biology and lived experience. Do our physical characteristics define us, or does the subjective experience take precedence? This redefinition of identity forces society to confront what truly constitutes humanity in a world where personal experience increasingly shapes reality.

Genetic research, such as CRISPR technology, deepens these questions. Scientists now wield the power to edit genes, offering hope for curing diseases and enhancing human capabilities. However, this progress also presents ethical dilemmas: Should we eliminate suffering, or does suffering play a role in the human experience? In pushing the boundaries of biology, are we creators or stewards, and what responsibility do we bear in reshaping life itself?

Design thinking adds another layer to this debate. Through the lens of intersectionality, it emphasizes the complexity of identity, shaped by overlapping factors like race, gender, and class. This approach challenges us to see identity not as static but as a fluid, evolving mosaic. Are we merely a product of external realities, or is there a deeper essence that defines who we are?

"All around the world, we have seen too many young people drowning in options, believing that identity is infinitely customizable. But with the option to customize one's identity, more choice leads to confusion, and isolation escalates with more autonomy." She notes, "Even when they hear Truth spoken in love, young people's first response is to fact-check it online. 'Let me see if this is true,' they say, opening ChatGPT or scrolling Google. There exists a fundamental distrust in authority and a loneliness that comes from carrying so much internally, with very few trustworthy voices to help them process." — *Ania Greenwood*

These explorations—AI, gender, genetic editing, and design—are not isolated debates, but central to society's ongoing struggle with human identity. The general human insecurity and lack of identity, brought on by the rapidly shifting definition of humanity, stems not only from our growing replaceability by machines, but also from the fluidity of our image—digitally through filters and avatars, and physically through augmentation and medical procedures. The more we stare at ourselves, the more we reinvent ourselves, the more we replace ourselves, the less we truly know who we are.

IMPACT ON JESUS-FOLLOWING

The Christian narrative often feels out of sync in places like Silicon Valley, where subjective experience and technological advancement shape the cultural landscape. The essence of the gospel is compromised when tradition, ritual, and personalities overshadow its core, particularly in a culture that sees humans as programmable beings shaped by external forces, rather than distinct creations of God. Culture asserts that we are born good but corrupted by oppression, and our purpose lies in self-expression and improving the world through social or technological progress.

In this context, the gospel's teaching about human uniqueness, rooted in our identity as image-bearers of God and our need for redemption, can feel foreign. As society's understanding of humanity continues to evolve, resistance grows toward what are perceived as outdated Christian traditions and expressions of the gospel.

THE EFFECT ON GOSPEL PROCLAMATION

When we deeply question what it means to be human, it inevitably forces us to re-examine our relationship with God. The resulting social and cultural shifts are significant, but even more profound is how these questions affect how people view the gospel. When individuals grapple with their identity and doubt their inherent value, it creates a disruptive unease. This disruption challenges their sense of self and purpose. However, living entirely apart from a connection with God is far more damaging. Such disconnection is destructive to their very being, leading to a fundamental loss of meaning and fulfillment.

To see this impact, let's review the basic gospel message:

• Creation: Humanity was created good, bearing the image of God, with an inherent purpose to reflect His nature.

• Fall: Sin distorted this image, introducing brokenness into both nature and humanity, resulting in separation from God.

• Redemption: Through Jesus Christ, we are reconciled to God and restored to our true identity.

• Restoration: In the fullness of time, God will renew all things—restoring humanity to its intended glory.

As cultural shifts continue and evolutionary theory persistently challenges the plausibility of the gospel—particularly the belief that God created the world— they influence how the gospel is understood and received. This, in turn, raises new questions about humanity itself. When the church speaks of sin and the need for reconciliation with God, many may struggle to see the relevance of this message in a world where technology promises to solve problems once thought to be intrinsic to the human condition. The idea that humans are broken, sinful, and in need of salvation can feel increasingly out of step with a culture that elevates personal authenticity and technological progress as the answers to our deepest needs. As a result, the appeal of the gospel often diminishes when the focus centers on sin and guilt.

The rise of AI, the normalization of diverse gender identities, and the promise of scientific advancement suggest a future where humans are not defined by any eternal standard but by what we can create or choose for ourselves. In this context, the Church's call to follow Christ and embrace abundant, eternal life often loses traction against society's manufactured expectation of a future shaped entirely by human design. The desirability of the gospel weakens when it is presented primarily as a warning of punishment and eternal damnation to a society convinced it holds control over its own destiny.

This is why the question of what it means to be human is so critical. It is not merely a philosophical inquiry; it is the lens through which the world is beginning to view the gospel. When humanity is defined by the power to shape its own identity, transcend its limitations, or reimagine its very nature, the traditional gospel message of creation, the fall, redemption, and restoration may seem increasingly distant and irrelevant, reducing the attractiveness of the gospel.

In a world where the definition of humanity is in flux, the gospel message has never been more countercultural, and yet, perhaps, it has never been more necessary. Necessity doesn't guarantee adoption. For the relevance of the gospel to be rediscovered, we must move beyond the guilt, shame, and punishment narrative that served the church well through the Industrial Revolution and two world wars, and return to a more ancient story—a simple message carried by first-century fishermen and Pharisees whose lives were forever changed by an encounter with Jesus. The gospel offers a radically different understanding of what it means to be human—one grounded in the eternal, unchanging truth of God's image and purpose.

SKILLS:

THE SKILL OF CLARITY

From the very beginning, humanity's struggle with identity and purpose has been at the heart of its spiritual journey. In Genesis 3, the enemy targeted Adam and Eve's understanding of who they were, distorting their relationship with God and the flourishing life He had designed for them. That same distortion persists today as we wrestle with the competing narratives that seek to redefine the very essence of humanity. In the process, we find ourselves entangled in arguments and philosophies that stray from God's original design, blinding us to the truth that He created us to live in the freedom of His grace and the fullness of relationship with Him.

In both Christian and secular spaces, there's a tendency to add layers—rituals, systems, and ideologies—to perfect our image or draw closer to God. But in truth, our purpose has always been rooted in unity with Him. The more we align with God's original intent for our lives, the more the complexities of this world, no matter how daunting, become less threatening. As humans living in a broken world, we experience the dis-ease of disconnection between our intended purpose and the fractured reality around us—further compounded by a broken sense of identity. The confusion and fluidity of humanity prey on this instability, suggesting mirage-like solutions. Yet when we discover the truth that transcends the very questions we wrestle with, we can thrive even in the midst of ambiguity.

Cultivating the skill of clarity is more crucial than seeking certainty. Clarity allows us to focus on the truths we can confidently affirm while acknowledging the mysteries of faith with humility. It frees us from needing to answer all the questions to propose the answers to the questions that really matter. It allows us to connect genuinely with a generation that values openness and authenticity over knowledge and authority. Clarity enables us to communicate the gospel without the unnecessary pomp, ceremony, or confusion

THE CHURCH'S *MISSION* IS NOT TO PROVIDE CERTAINTY FOR EVERY QUESTION BUT TO *CLARIFY* WHERE IT MATTERS MOST.

that can sometimes obscure its simplicity. A pure focus on Jesus—the prototype of our original design and restorer of our relationship with God—is the gospel, the Good News. When we offer clear, unadulterated truth, we create space for others to experience the life-changing reality of God's grace through encountering Jesus, while still grappling with questions and navigating ambiguity in an ever-evolving world.

Clarity requires acknowledging our limits. Society is increasingly uncertain and complex, and presenting a false certainty only adds to the noise. By admitting we don't have all the answers, we offer a more authentic witness that invites trust and engagement. Knowing what we know—and admitting what we don't—invites others who lack all the answers to join us on the journey of faith.

The Church's mission is not to provide certainty for every question but to clarify where it matters most. Clarity on the gospel's eternal truths can cut through the noise and offer hope, serving as an anchor in the storm. This generation does not need more opinions or rigid dogmas. They need an authentic expression of God's love, rooted in humility and delivered clearly.

We are not suggesting that the answer to all the complexity, convoluted emotion, and infinitely deep philosophical conundrum of the definition of humanity is answered in the simple idea of clarity. Rather, we suggest that while humanity wrestles with these questions, Christian leaders should focus on presenting a clear and compelling message built upon the unshakable foundations of the faith—without getting lost in our own crows' nest of rituals or tangled spaghetti bowl of dogma.

The closer we walk in step with God's original design, the less intimidating the world's complexities become, no matter how daunting they may appear. This is because clarity serves as an anchor in the storm of identity confusion, freeing us from the need to answer every question and allowing us to focus on the truths that matter most.

CLARIFYING IDENTITY AMIDST AMBIGUITY

Amid uncertainty, what truths must remain clear? Only a powerful narrative of humanity's transcendent, eternal identity can cut through the shifting, ever-evolving debate over what it means to be human.

The truth is that the Creator alone defines His creation, and our highest human identity transcends humanity itself, beginning with His divinity. This reality is indispensable in communicating the gospel, especially in an age that relentlessly challenges and reexamines the nature of humanity.

We must begin by recognizing that human identity is inherently complex, consisting of interconnected components that shape who we are. To understand and clarify our identity, we must first consider the factors that influence its expression:

• Association: With whom do I identify?

• Actions: What actions define me?

• Nature: What inherent qualities do I possess (DNA, biology, lineage)?

• Nurture: What experiences have shaped me?

These elements intertwine to shape our sense of self and the expression of our identity. The family and culture into which we are born shape us, while the relationships and connections fostered over time both nurture and define us. Our particular strengths and traits emerge from innate abilities combined with our choices. Our skills and actions—whether in work, art, or personal decisions—further distinguish us. The biological and genetic makeup provides the foundation upon which our experiences and actions shape our identity.

Like an intricate, complicated recipe with multiple ingredients, steps, and processes, our perception and expression of self are carefully formed over time. Elements out of our control, like nature and upbringing, mix with factors under our control, like decisions and activities, to create an innate blend of forces and personal influences that craft the complex tapestry that makes up who we are.

If you call yourself a cake, you could describe the parts: cake layers, icing, and decorations. Or you could explain the ingredients (flour, sugar & eggs) and processes that brought it about (mixed, baked, whipped). And though that would help understand the cake, essentially, the cake is more than just ingredients and processes. It is wheat, cream, and at an even higher level, carbon, chemical elements, and at the highest level, atoms.

In the same way, much of the debate, confusion, and argument over what it means to be human revolves around perceptions, descriptions, ingredients, and processes yet never addresses the core of the human identity at its highest level: our origin. We have been created in the image of God, and though that image was marred by sin, Jesus came to display and restore our true identity.

Ania shared a powerful story—one that captures both the depth of the crisis and the hope of restoration. A twelve-year-old girl, feeling discomfort in her body during puberty, turned to the internet for answers. An algorithm immediately and confidently told her, "You are trans," and she embraced that identity. Over the years, she pursued transition—first socially, then hormonally, and eventually through surgery, building a life and career as a man. Externally, she was building a new identity as a man, and it looked as though she had found herself. Yet internally, something still felt wrong, as if the truth still eluded her. At 22, overwhelmed by despair, she collapsed onto her sofa, ready to give up. Then something happened. She described it as a warm wind—an overwhelming sense of love—filling the room. A voice asked her, gently but clearly: "Do you want to know the truth?" She said yes. And the voice replied, "You are a woman."

That moment transformed her. Overcome with unexplainable peace, she began a journey back to herself—and ultimately to Jesus. She joined a church and a Bible study called *Who Am I?*, where she discovered her identity, not as something self-created, but as something received, rooted in Christ. She has found fulfillment in her identity in Christ, and invests her time in helping others navigate the complexities of identity in today's world. Her story stands as a stark reminder that opportunities for augmentation can magnify the brokenness of gender confusion many times over. Never before in history has this challenge been quite so great or its impact so far-reaching.

I was deeply impacted by Ania sharing this story with humility and conviction. For her, it's not about debating ideologies—it's about loving people back to truth. Too many adults, she said, are afraid to speak the truth out loud. They say, "Just be happy," or "Do what feels right," and step back. But this generation doesn't need passive freedom. They need anchored freedom. She's seen too many young people drowning in options, believing that identity is infinitely customizable. But more choices have brought more confusion, and greater autonomy has led to greater isolation. Some changes, like surgery or hormone therapy, are irreversible, and when regret hits, the weight is crushing.

But there is hope. There is a voice of truth that still speaks. There is a Jesus who restores. And there is a generation—wounded but searching—that is still longing for purpose.

WHAT TO BE CLEAR ABOUT?

While many forces impact us, we can find true identity in Christ at the core of our being. By cultivating the skill of clarity, we can present the gospel not as a rigid set of rules or behaviors, but as an invitation to discover the truest self—the person God created us to be. Recognizing that amidst shifting currents of technological advancements, social movements, and scientific discoveries, this core truth anchors us amidst life's complexities and provides stability as outer variables shift over time.

To enhance the clarity that the gospel holds in an ever-updating digitized society effectively, the Church must focus on three transcendent truths:

1. **The Image of God**
   Humanity is created in the image of God (Gen 1:26-27)—not in the image of work, knowledge, or feelings. This divine truth provides clarity amid uncertainty. When we embrace our humanity, illuminated by God's infallible divinity, we help others navigate their struggle to define themselves in a world increasingly shaped by artificial intelligence (AI) and digital distortion. AI may outpace human intelligence, but it will never surpass the wisdom or sovereignty of God. As a Church, we must be

a beacon of hope, affirming that God defines our value and purpose.

2. **The Spiritual Reality**
   Humanity is not merely rational or emotional; we are also spiritual. If the church shies away from emphasizing the spiritual dimension, we risk losing an entire generation. Rational arguments or practical steps may appeal momentarily, but they cannot compete with the transcendent reality of knowing God and being known by Him. As John 17:3 reminds us, "This is eternal life: to know God." This spiritual truth remains unshaken by the rapid pace of change or societal uncertainties.

3. **The Eternal Perspective**
   While technological and societal changes may feel overwhelming, the church's hope is rooted in eternity. No matter how advanced AI becomes or how divided society grows, these things are fleeting. As followers of Christ, we are part of a kingdom that transcends this world. Even if humanity faces a dystopian future, our identity and purpose remain secure in God's eternal reality. The gospel calls us to live for what does not perish and build a foundation for what will endure forever.

We must embrace the gospel's transcendent, mystical fullness and present it with humble, human clarity. The more we reflect God's glory in the way we live and love, the more we help others see themselves through His eyes. However, if we present the gospel in an overly simplistic, purely rational way—presenting ourselves as having it all figured out—the inauthenticity of our false security and so-called "certainty" will cause others to resist the gospel, dismissing it as just another opinion.

THE CALL TO RELATIONSHIP

As the world grapples with questions of identity, the gospel offers a compelling vision of what it means to be human—a vision rooted in a relationship with God, empowered by Christ's redemption, and illuminated by the Holy Spirit. In a time when innovation often overshadows introspection, the gospel invites humanity to pause, reflect, and return to its Creator. By accepting this invitation, we step into the fullest expression of what it means to be human—rooted in eternal hope and anchored in a purpose that rises above every cultural tide, scientific breakthrough, and technological shift.

Just like with Adam and Eve after the fall, struggling with their sense of self while God walked in the garden searching after them, in the same way, God is still pursuing us amid today's identity confusion. As we navigate the complexities and uncertainties of who we are and why we exist in the 21st century, He does not leave us to wander alone in our nakedness and shame. He comes searching for us, calling us back into the relationship, and offering us the covering of His grace. He does not simply provide a list of answers or a set of rules; He walks with us, listens to our questions, and gently guides us toward truth. In a world increasingly defined by artificial intelligence and technological advancements, the gospel reminds us that our true identity is found not in what we create or achieve but in the image of God in which we are made. This divine image gives us inherent value, dignity, and purpose, providing a firm foundation upon which we can confidently build our lives and face the future.

A note on this chapter: The core concepts and initial framework of "Shifting Definition of Being Human" were significantly shaped by the writing and insights of Matthew Niermann. His contribution was foundational to its development.

Read more about Matthew in the "Contributors" section in the back of this book.

CHAPTER 3 SUMMARY

This chapter explores the profound and accelerating shifts in how humanity defines itself, driven by technological advances like AI and biotechnology, as well as evolving social movements. It notes that past definitions of humanity have centered on survival, creation, thought, feeling, and creativity, but AI can now replicate many of these functions. This leaves a generation facing an identity crisis—asking not only "Who am I?" but also "Why am I like this?" The chapter argues that the church's mission is to bring clarity to the confusion by pointing to a transcendent truth: our identity is grounded in being created in the image of God. By clearly presenting this eternal reality, the church can anchor hope and purpose in a world where humanity's very essence feels increasingly uncertain.

SKILL:
EXPEDITE CLARITY IN UNCERTAINTY

REFLECTIVE QUESTIONS

1. Where in your ministry or personal life might you conflate clarity with certainty?

2. What are you doing to help the next generation find clarity amid cultural confusion?

3. What does it mean for you to lead with both humility and conviction in this identity-shifting world?

JOIN THE CONVERSATION
& WATCH THE INTERVIEWS HERE

PEOPLE
DON'T NEED
PASSIVE
FREEDOM.
THEY NEED
ANCHORED
FREEDOM.

ANIA GREENWOOD

TECHNOLOGY ITSELF
IS A BLANK SLATE.
IT IS NEITHER
GOOD NOR BAD.

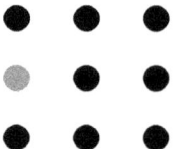

CHAPTER 4

SHIFTING DELINEATIONS OF DIGITAL EXISTENCE

Our digital lives are not just a tool but a defining aspect of our reality, reshaping how we communicate, form our identities, and even perceive truth. This chapter explores how the new landscape of digital existence further exacerbates the internal identity crisis, leaving us feeling both connected and fragmented at the same time.

Along the winding Ituí River, deep within the emerald embrace of the Brazilian Amazon, lives the Marubo.[1] Their world, for generations, was woven from the hunt, the catch, and stories passed down by word of mouth. Connection to anything beyond their verdant sanctuary was a whisper on a crackling amateur radio, a message painstakingly relayed from one village to the next. Then came the future. In 2022, twenty Starlink satellite antennas descended into their remote existence, instantly obliterating a chasm of isolation that had spanned centuries. What unfolded next was a lightning-fast lesson in the raw, unbridled power of digital existence—an amplifier and accelerator that, in its neutrality, could unleash both dazzling promise and unforeseen chaos.[1]

At first, a wave of widespread happiness and optimism swept through the community.[1] The internet, they believed, was a divine intervention, a direct line to life-saving aid in emergencies, a gateway to education, and a bridge to distant relatives. And for a time, it was. Starlink delivered, undeniably. Lives were saved, literally, with instantaneous calls for help in critical situations like venomous snake bites. Online lessons opened up new horizons for children, and the Marubo found a powerful platform to share their vibrant culture with the world, even utilizing it to report the relentless creep of illegal deforestation, guarding their ancestral lands.[1]

But the honeymoon was brutally short. A mere nine months into this digital revolution, cracks began to show—familiar echoes of problems faced by modern households: teenagers glued to phones; group chats full of gossip; addictive social networks and rampant use of pornography.[1] Elders watched, heartbroken, as young people abandoned traditional communal activities for the seductive glow of screens. Group chats, once a novelty, festered with gossip and, more disturbingly, for sharing explicit content—a practice unprecedented in their culture. The very fabric of their daily lives, the sacred routines of hunting, fishing, and planting, were disrupted. A stark generational divide emerged; the elders were filled with profound worry for their culture, while the young embraced new aspirations, dreaming of modern careers beyond the village. This neutral technology, the internet, has amplified both connection and isolation, education and distraction, empowerment and vulnerability. It even armed the very criminals threatening their lands, with illegal miners exploiting Starlink to coordinate their illicit operations and evade authorities.

The Marubo's journey became a visceral demonstration of confronting the internet's potential and peril all at once.[1] They navigated in less than one year what modern societies grappled with over decades.[1] This "compressed modernity" plunged them into the deep end without the gradual, generational shaping of societal norms, unwritten rules, or formal regulations that other cultures had developed over time. Yet, what truly sets the Marubo apart is their unwavering resilience. They weren't passive victims. Recognizing the disquieting shifts, their leaders took decisive action, implementing strict time limits for internet usage, literally switching it off for hours at a time. During crucial community gatherings, they demanded that the internet be disconnected, ensuring their internal governance and conversations remained sacred and free from digital interference. They are, emphatically, the architects of their own digital destiny, asserting their agency in the face of profound technological change.

The Marubo's story isn't just a fascinating anthropological account; it's a mirror held up to us all. Their accelerated immersion into the digital realm screams a fundamental truth: technology itself is a blank slate. It is neither good nor bad. It is a powerful accelerant, a catalyst that simply magnifies the existing currents of human nature and the structures of our societies. The profound impact of digital existence—whether it lifts us to new heights or plunges us into unforeseen depths—hinges entirely on our intent, our awareness, and how skillfully we learn to engage with it. As we journey into the *Shifting Delineations of Digital Existence*, the Marubo teach us a vital lesson: "the ball we cannot see" is not merely the dazzling technology itself, but the immense, neutral power it wields, and our urgent, collective responsibility to learn how to play the game on our own terms.

A WORLD-HISTORIC SHIFT

The Marubo's experience, while unique in its compressed timeline, is a microcosm of a much larger, world-historic change that is reshaping global society. We are currently living through a period of transformative shifts, comparable in scale to pivotal junctures in history, such as the post-World War II era, the aftermath of the Civil War, or even the Enlightenment that birthed the modern world. These periods are characterized by tipping points where slowly developing technologies suddenly become mainstream and indispensable, leading to significant societal upheaval and polarization as old systems break down and new ones emerge. Historically, these transformative bursts of widespread innovation tend to occur in roughly 80-year cycles, each lasting about 21 years.[2]

SHIFTS:

As Peter Leyden suggests in his video "2025: The end of our world as we know it," we are on the cusp of a "world-historic change" driven by three interconnected technological tipping points:[3]

1. **The Dawn of Artificial Intelligence (AI):** The launch of generative AI tools like ChatGPT 3.5 in late 2022 marked a "world-historic moment," signaling the true

beginning of the "Age of AI." This is not merely an incremental advancement but a foundational shift, akin to the Bronze or Iron Age, in its capacity to amplify human mental powers exponentially, much as mechanical engines amplified physical capabilities. For the Church, this demands a critical examination of how AI will redefine creativity, truth, and even the nature of human intellect. How do we leverage AI for mission and ministry while upholding theological integrity and human dignity? How do we discern truth in an age of deepfakes and algorithmic biases? These are not distant concerns but immediate challenges for our digital existence.[3]

2. **The Abundance of Clean Energy:** While seemingly less directly "digital," the clean energy revolution, particularly in solar and battery technology, profoundly impacts our digital future. Unlike finite commodities, clean energy is a technology, meaning its cost can consistently decrease with increased production. This trend toward abundant and continuously cheaper energy will power the ever-growing demands of our digital infrastructure, from data centers and cloud computing to the myriad of connected devices that define our digital lives. A world with near-limitless, affordable energy opens up new possibilities for global connectivity, equitable access to digital resources, and sustainable digital practices, each of which has implications for how the Church engages with and serves a digitally interconnected world.[3]

3. **The Frontiers of Bioengineering (Synthetic Biology):** Around the same time as early generative AI breakthroughs, CRISPR technology emerged, allowing for the cheap and easy editing of any living being's genome. This enables unprecedented control over biological outcomes, from growing meat from animal cells in a vat, to the plummeting cost of sequencing the human genome. As the digital and biological lines blur, the implications for human identity, ethics, and even the definition of life itself are staggering. This directly intersects with the *Shifting Definition of Being Human* explored in Chapter 3. How will the Church minister to individuals whose biological realities are increasingly shaped by digital design? What theological frameworks are needed to navigate a future where human biology can be "engineered"?[3]

These technological shifts are not isolated phenomena but foundational elements for a larger societal reinvention—building a 21st-century civilization. This includes potential shifts from financial capitalism to sustainable capitalism, from representative democracy to digital democracy, and even from nation-states to some form of global governance to coordinate a world of 10 billion people. For the Church, this means recognizing that our digital existence is not a separate sphere but an integral part of this grand reinvention. The relevance deficit we face is exacerbated by our inability to grasp and respond to these monumental shifts fully.

MORE THAN AI

Morgan Stanley's presentation, "AI is about to get Physical," offers fascinating insights into Embodied AI.[4] The firm highlights that AI's rapid advancements are extending far beyond familiar digital screens and conversational interfaces. We are now witnessing the burgeoning field of embodied AI, where artificial intelligence transcends software and integrates directly into the physical world through advanced robotics and autonomous machines.[5]

Embodied AI refers to machines that possess the capacity to perceive the world, learn from it, navigate complex physical spaces, and even manipulate objects within three-dimensional reality. This includes everything from the autonomous vehicles already on our roads to the development of sophisticated humanoid robots. The driving force behind this revolution is the "race for photons": the critical need to collect and process vast amounts of real-world visual data to train "vision language actuation models." Just as a fruit fly learns efficient physical interaction through its biological design, embodied AI leverages hyper-realistic digital twins and physics engines for simulation, constantly narrowing the "sim-to-real" gap by incorporating recent, high-value real-world data.

This physical manifestation of AI promises to transform sectors ranging from transportation—through autonomous cars, low-altitude electric vertical take-off and landing aircraft (eVTOLs), and sophisticated drone swarms—to the global labor market, where humanoid robots are expected to take on dull, dirty, and dangerous tasks. Companies like Waymo, Meta (through its Reality Labs[6] and data-collecting devices), Amazon (with its growing use of robotics in fulfillment centers), Apple (leveraging in-car data), and Tesla (combining data, robotics, and energy solutions) are at the forefront of this physical AI revolution, pushing the boundaries of what automated machines can achieve.

For the Church, the rise of embodied AI deepens the questions around what it means to be human in a technologically advanced world. As machines increasingly mimic and augment human physical capabilities and interactions, the lines between the artificial and the authentically human will continue to blur. This intensifies the *Identity Insecurity* we've already discussed and places further urgency on how we balance digital and personal connection and redefine relationships in a digital world. Understanding this next frontier of AI is critical for leaders to truly grasp "the ball we cannot see" and discern how to faithfully navigate and minister within a world where intelligence is not only digital, but increasingly physically embodied.

THE ATTENTION ECONOMY

The term was first articulated by Nobel Laureate Herbert A. Simon in the late 1960s or early 1970s.[7] Simon, a psychologist and economist, presciently characterized the problem of information overload as an economic challenge. He observed that in a world rich with information, the true scarcity lay in what that information consumed: the attention of its recipients. His insight was remarkable. He predicted a future where the value of information itself would approach zero, while the value of attention would steadily increase.

The internet's advent in the mid-1990s marked a significant inflection point, dramatically accelerating this trend. As digital data began to double approximately every two years, information became incredibly cheap and ubiquitous, causing the "price of attention" to rise sharply. Building on Simon's foundational work, Thomas H. Davenport and John C. Beck formalized the "economics of attention" in 2001, defining it as an approach that explicitly treats human attention as a scarce commodity. Their influential 2002 book, The Attention Economy: Understanding the New Currency of Business, underscored that managing attention had become paramount for business success.[8] Around the same time, Michael Goldhaber further advanced the discourse, arguing that the attention economy represented a fundamental departure from the industrial, money-market-based economy, with its own distinct forms of wealth and class divisions. This intellectual trajectory—from Simon's initial observation to Goldhaber's articulation of a new economic order—reveals a deepening understanding of this pervasive, and often manipulative, economic system.

For the Church in the 21st century, the scarcity of attention presents the greatest frontier, much as Bible distribution and missional advancement into unreached people groups were for the global Church in the 20th century. In a time-poor society, where digital distractions endlessly compete for every moment of focus, the ability to genuinely capture and sustain the attention and engagement of individuals is paramount. This isn't just about cutting through the noise; it's about re-envisioning how the gospel is presented and experienced in a way that resonates deeply amidst the pervasive forces of the attention economy, inviting rather than demanding, and cultivating presence in a world of constant fragmentation.

IN A TIME-POOR SOCIETY, THE ABILITY TO GENUINELY CAPTURE AND SUSTAIN THE ATTENTION AND ENGAGEMENT OF INDIVIDUALS IS PARAMOUNT.

IMPACT ON JESUS-FOLLOWING:

Existence in the digital age revolves around three essential truths: digitization is neutral, authenticity is critical, and relationships remain central. By understanding and applying these principles, we can effectively navigate the complexities of the digital world.

TECHNOLOGY AND THE CHURCH

Balancing digital tools and personal connections is crucial in all fields. While technology can improve efficiency, it cannot replace the human empathy needed for positive outcomes, much like how a perfect cup of coffee blends the right beans (technology) with skillful brewing (personal care). The Church faces a pivotal moment. Failure to adapt to societal shifts may lead to a loss of trust and relevance. Once rooted in shared experiences, trust is now influenced by new factors, particularly in the digital age—more about this in a later chapter.

For Kevin Lee, a leading China marketing strategist, consumer-centric innovation expert, and founder of the Purpose Accelerator, the future is already unfolding, and it's digital, disorienting, and deeply human. With over 15 years advising Fortune 500 executives through China Youthology and more than two decades coaching individuals to discover their identity and purpose, Kevin is immersed in the tension between technological advancement and spiritual identity. The world is being reshaped not only by devices and algorithms, but by a shift in what it means to be human. "Today's generation isn't just digital-native," Kevin said. "They're social media natives living in a multiverse of personas."

Today's primary challenge is the rise of second-generation digital natives—children of tech-savvy parents—driving technological change. This shift impacts generational relationships and accelerates digital tool integration into everyday life. TV once disrupted family connections. In the 90s, a family watching a television program together was considered disruptive to family life compared to sitting around the dinner table. Today's norm is for every family member to watch something different on their device of choice, creating fragmented media consumption, where there is not even a shared experience of the same media.

> **TODAY'S GENERATION ISN'T JUST DIGITALLY NATIVE; THEY'RE SOCIAL MEDIA NATIVES LIVING IN A MULTIVERSE OF PERSONAS.**
>
> **KEVIN LEE**

Advancements in AI and virtual reality raise concerns about identity and self-perception, presenting challenges and opportunities for the Church. While embracing these tools creatively, it's essential to maintain authentic human connections. These technological shifts reflect broader societal changes in media consumption and interactions, urging the Church to rethink and reckon with the reality of how the gospel can be shared in a more individualized, disconnected world.

This transformation challenges traditional concepts of trust, community, authority, and humanity.

NAVIGATING SUPPLY AND DEMAND IN THE DIGITAL AGE

The fundamental economic principle of supply and demand dictates that when demand for a resource is high and its supply is low, the price or value of that resource increases due to its scarcity. This concept provides a powerful lens through which to understand the evolving digital landscape and its impact on what society values. As we journey through recent history, we can identify three distinct "ages" where the nature of scarcity has shifted, fundamentally altering the dynamics of supply and demand, particularly within the realm of information and technology.

1. The First Age: The Scarcity of Information

There was a time, not long ago, when information itself was a scarce commodity. In this era, individuals and institutions that possessed specialized knowledge or access to information held significant power and influence. People would willingly pay a premium to acquire information, whether through formal education, purchasing books, or belonging to exclusive groups. The advent of the internet began to disrupt this model, as it was initially built around the value derived from this very scarcity of information. Data companies and the dot-com boom were fueled by their ability to provide access to previously hard-to-reach information. In this age, the demand for information was high, and its relatively limited supply ensured its considerable value.

2. The Second Age: The Scarcity of Application

The digital revolution did not stop at merely making information accessible; it began to automate its availability. As information became increasingly abundant and democratized, its inherent scarcity—and therefore its intrinsic value—diminished. Today, the average individual possesses more information readily available on their smartphone than world leaders had access to just a few decades ago.

This shift gave rise to the "Age of Application." With information readily available, the new scarcity, and thus the new locus of value, became the tools and platforms that could effectively organize, interpret, and apply this vast ocean of data. The popular phrase "there's an app for that" encapsulated this era. The focus was on specific applications designed for specific tasks, providing efficient ways to navigate and utilize information. For a time, educational communities and businesses thrived by demonstrating how to apply information, offering credentials that validated this ability. Downloading a particular app or learning a specific way of doing things held value because it provided a scarce means of practical application in a world overflowing with raw data.

3. The Third Age: The Scarcity of Interaction and Experience

Just as the scarcity of information was eroded by its automation, the scarcity of its application is now facing a similar transformation, driven mainly by the rise of artificial intelligence. AI has begun to automate the very applications that once held premium value. This ushers us into a new, third age: the "Age of Interaction and Experience Scarcity."

In a world where both information and the means to apply it are becoming increasingly abundant and automated, genuine human interaction and unique, meaningful experiences are emerging as the new scarce resources. The value proposition is shifting from merely knowing or doing something to being with and experiencing something. Opportunities now lie not in trying to recreate the scarcity of information or application—those battles have largely been lost to technological progress. Instead, the challenge and the opportunity reside in fostering and facilitating meaningful interactions and creating valuable experiences. This is the new frontier—where demand is growing, supply remains relatively limited, and value commands a premium in our evolving digital society.

Understanding these three ages of scarcity provides a crucial framework for individuals and organizations, particularly those in education and ministry, to adapt and remain relevant. The focus must shift from guarding information or delivering applications to cultivating interaction and designing transformative experiences—the new scarce resources people are longing for. It is in this human-centric space that true value will be found and created in the years to come.

The tectonic shifts in digital existence are not merely reshaping society; they are profoundly altering the landscape of faith, particularly for those striving to follow Jesus. The Church, like the Marubo, is confronting both the immense potential and inherent perils of this new digital reality. Understanding these impacts is crucial for navigating the future of faith.

AGES OF SCARCITY

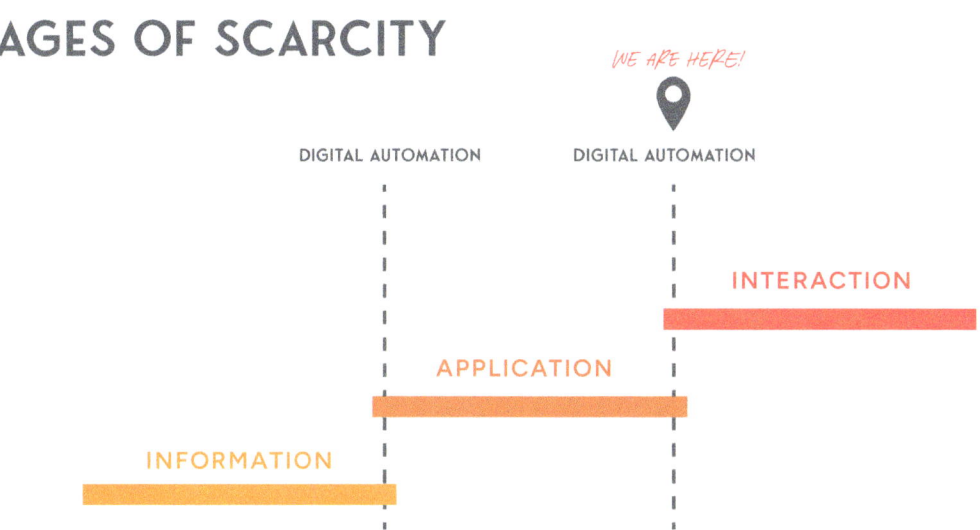

THE CONFUSION OF ARTIFICIAL AND SUPERNATURAL: MISUNDERSTANDING ONE FOR THE OTHER

In an increasingly sophisticated digital world, where AI can simulate empathy and virtual realities can feel incredibly real, a critical challenge for Jesus-followers is discerning the boundary between the artificial and the supernatural. As Kevin Lee points out, "AI can simulate empathy, but it can't deliver revelation." There's a subtle but significant risk of mistaking technologically induced experiences or carefully curated digital interactions for genuine spiritual encounters or authentic community. This confusion can lead to a shallow faith, where convenience and curated comfort are prioritized over the challenging, yet deeply formative, aspects of genuine spiritual growth that often require conflict, compromise, and yielding—elements that AI companions are explicitly designed to avoid.

A fascinating paradox is emerging within the younger generations: the "digital natives" and "social media natives" of Gen Z, who seamlessly navigate online multiverses of personas, are often drawn back to the physicality of the Bible.[9] While digital Bibles offer unparalleled accessibility and search functions, there's a growing appreciation for the tangible, tactile experience of holding a physical book, underlining passages, and encountering scripture in a less fragmented, screen-dependent manner.[9] This "digital rebellion" isn't a rejection of technology, but perhaps a subconscious yearning for something authentic and unchanging in a fluid digital world. It highlights a tension where the convenience of digital tools meets a deeper human need for grounding and a singular focus, contrasting with the fragmented attention demanded by constant digital engagement. For the Church, this presents an opportunity to bridge the digital and physical, recognizing that while digital platforms can open doors, the enduring power of the Word often resonates profoundly in its physical form.

REDEFINITION OF CONNECTEDNESS: MANY FACEBOOK FRIENDS, FEW REAL ONES

The digital age has fundamentally redefined what it means to be "connected." We can have thousands of "friends" or followers on social media, yet experience profound loneliness and isolation. This dichotomy is particularly acute for younger generations, where a teenager might find it easier to text their deepest feelings than to articulate them face-to-face, or where connection within a gaming community feels more accessible than navigating complex family dynamics. The emergence of phenomena like "Japanese fake friends" or "hired friends" underscores a deeper societal yearning for genuine connection amidst widespread isolation.

Compounding this, the missing millennial generation, in many contexts, creates a significant gap in translation and bridge-building between older and younger generations.[10] This generational disconnect hinders the Church's ability to minister effectively across the digital divide, as traditional concepts of community and relationship often clash with the digital-first realities of younger believers. The challenge for Jesus-followers is not just to understand this redefinition, but to intentionally cultivate real, face-to-face relationships that offer the depth, accountability, and transformative friction that digital connections often lack.

COMPETITION FOR FOCUSED ATTENTION: THE OVERWHELMED AND DISENGAGED

In a world saturated with information and constant digital stimulation, focused attention has become the new scarce resource. People have limited airtime, and the escalating intensity in competition for people's time means that every app, every influencer, every piece of content is vying for precious "eyes on." For the Church, this presents a significant hurdle: how does the gospel, often presented in information-centric ways, cut through the incessant noise?

The constant bombardment of data can lead to feelings of being "overwhelmed and disengaged." An information-centric gospel presentation, which might have thrived in the *Age of Information Scarcity,* risks getting lost in the deluge of digital content. The challenge is not just to be heard, but to resonate deeply enough to capture and sustain attention amidst a landscape of infinite distractions. This requires a shift from merely delivering information to fostering experiences and interactions that are compelling enough to cut through the digital clutter and genuinely engage individuals in a meaningful way.

DEMOCRATIZATION OF INFORMATION:
LOWERING BARRIERS, EXPANDING REACH

While posing challenges, the digital age also offers unprecedented opportunities for the spread of the gospel through the "democratization of information." Barriers that once seemed insurmountable—geographic distance, language differences, and limited access to resources—are being dismantled. The Masai Mara, a tribe in one of the most renowned National Reserves in Kenya, illustrates this phenomenon of the expanding reach of technology.[11] In the heart of the wildlife-dense plains that host the Great Migration of wildebeests and zebras each year, a safari guide is armed with a cellphone, illustrating how individuals in previously remote areas can now have access to and share information globally.[11]

Language barriers are being removed through translation tools, allowing the gospel message to traverse cultures with greater ease. Crucially, this places the "majority world" on a more equal footing in how the gospel is shared and received. No longer are traditional centers of influence the sole custodians of theological knowledge or ministry strategies. Digital tools empower local leaders, facilitate peer-to-peer learning, and allow the gospel to spread organically in ways previously unimaginable. This democratization compels the Church to embrace a more decentralized, collaborative approach to global missions, recognizing that the Spirit moves freely through all who are equipped and connected in the digital age.

SKILLS:

DIGITIZATION: A NEUTRAL REALITY

Digitization has become a defining force of our era. It is essential to recognize that digitization, like money, is inherently neutral. Money is a tool—a means to an end—and so is digitization. Neither is inherently good nor bad; their impact is determined by how they are used. Money itself is not the root of all evil, despite common misquotes. The Bible reminds us that "the love of money is the root of all evil," not money itself. Similarly, when digital tools become our masters, they lead to harm; yet, when they serve as instruments in our hands, they can accomplish tremendous good. Technology is not the enemy, but it must be used with wisdom and seen as an invitation, not a replacement.

Jesus' teaching that we "cannot serve both God and mammon" emphasizes the danger of misplaced worship. Just as money makes a terrible master but a great servant, digitization can be a terrible master, leading to addiction, superficiality, and broken relationships. Consider how digitization has transformed the ministry. Bible translations that once took decades can now be completed in years. Previously resistant to the gospel, closed countries are increasingly permeable to Christian influence through digital connections. Social media, livestreaming, and messaging platforms allow the Church to reach corners of the world that would otherwise remain untouched, showing that the future may be digital, but the gospel remains incarnational.

However, the same tools that connect us can also harm us. Social media can magnify the gospel's message or break lives by fueling addiction, comparison, and misinformation. The tools themselves remain neutral; how we wield them matters. This understanding is the first foundational principle for digital existence: Digitization is a tool, and we must use it wisely for the glory of God.

The same fire that cooks the food burns down the house.

A tool that can be used for good or ill. Its impact depends on our intentionality, particularly for a generation that views the digital world as their natural environment.

AUTHENTICITY IN THE DIGITAL SPACE

The rise of digitization has also reshaped our understanding of authenticity. As the world becomes more digital, the need for authenticity grows. Previous generations often viewed digital interactions as less "real" and genuine than physical ones, associating authenticity with face-to-face communication. However, younger generations—those born into a digital-first world—see the digital and physical as equally authentic.

Kevin is seeing a new kind of fragmentation—one that stretches beyond scattered thoughts or scattered time. It's the fragmentation of the self. Young people are managing multiple accounts, personas, and carefully curated versions of themselves across platforms. And while these fractured identities allow them to explore, they leave little room for integration. Kevin explains that the next generation is picking up pieces everywhere, not knowing how all these fragments of identity fit together. He says, "They know they're authentic—but they still don't know who they are." The result isn't inauthenticity—it's exhaustion. A quiet existential ache. This generation isn't pretending to be someone they're not. They just don't know how to make sense of all the versions of who they are.

DIGITIZATION IS A TOOL, AND WE MUST USE IT WISELY FOR THE GLORY OF GOD.

This generational evolution underscores a profound cultural shift. For many younger individuals, authenticity is defined more by the message than the medium. They evaluate authenticity based on transparency, consistency, and meaningful connection, whether online or in person. Leaders and organizations must adapt to this new paradigm by learning to communicate authentically in digital spaces.

GENERATIONAL ENGAGEMENT WITH DIGITAL TECHNOLOGY HAS EVOLVED:[12]

- The first users, the digital explorers, approached the digital world with curiosity, experiencing things like the first PCs or virtual reality for the first time.[12]

- Next came the digital immigrants, largely comprised of Gen Xers and Baby Boomers, who adapted to the digital environment later in life.[12]

- Their children became digital natives, growing up with the internet as an integral part of their daily existence. This generation views the digital world as their natural environment. A study even revealed that some teenagers ranked the internet as a priority over water, listing basic needs as air, internet, water, and food.[12]

Today, we are witnessing the emergence of a second generation of digital natives. Unlike their parents, these children are not teaching older generations about digital tools; instead, their parents are teaching them. This shift highlights how deeply ingrained the digital world has become. The divide between physical and digital authenticity no longer exists for this generation.

This new reality requires learning how to appear authentic in digital spaces. Research consistently points to the importance of authenticity for younger generations. Digital authenticity demands vulnerability, consistency, and intentionality, allowing for genuine connections in spaces that may seem impersonal at first glance.

RELATIONSHIPS IN A DIGITAL WORLD

At its core, the gospel is about relationships—our connection with God and one another. This truth transcends time and technology, anchoring ministry in the unchanging need for human connection. While the tools and methods of ministry evolve, shaped by technological advances like the digital world, the heart of ministry remains rooted in fostering authentic relationships.

The rise of digital spaces introduces new ways to connect, offering tools that can bridge physical distances and reach people in unprecedented ways. Yet, even as these tools become integral to modern life, the ultimate goal remains unchanged: human-to-human engagement. Digital platforms, while facilitating connection, are tools to enhance the depth and authenticity of genuine relationships, not to replace them. In every era, including our own, the gospel calls us to prioritize the relational heart of ministry, wisely using all available means to strengthen the connections that define life and faith.

Throughout history, every significant move of God has used the tools of its time to further the gospel. For example, the Jesus Revolution thrived in informal spaces like coffee shops, while great revivals used the organ or other innovations in worship. Modern worship movements use lights, sound, and technology to create engaging environments. Today, digital tools like AI, augmented reality, and social media represent the next frontier, adding another layer of complexity—and danger. Kevin warns that AI companions are quickly becoming the closest "relationships" for millions, particularly in places like China, where AI boyfriends and AI girlfriends are among the top search terms. "These agents are built to serve us, agree with us, mirror us," Kevin said. "But in doing so, they erase something deeply human—conflict and compromise."

In real relationships—with parents, spouses, friends—conflict is inevitable, and compromise is essential. But as people turn more and more to agreeable AI companions, Kevin worries that we're losing the very friction that shapes us. "What does it mean to be human," he asked, "if we never need to yield, forgive, or grow through resistance?"

The pandemic highlighted the potential of digital spaces to facilitate relationships. What once seemed like impersonal tools—Zoom meetings, virtual worship, social media—became lifelines for community and faith. Yet, the challenge remains: how can we ensure these connections translate into deep, lasting spiritual relationships? Digital tools should enhance, not replace, human connection.

Kevin remains hopeful. He's creating digital spaces—like the Purpose Accelerator—that help people rediscover themselves not apart from technology, but through it. The platform encourages deep reflection and personal discovery, and it's resonating. Participants, many not Christian, report powerful experiences: "I finally heard my own voice," some say. They describe not just engaging content, but a space that feels deeply human. It's not just the tech—it's the design. Kevin incorporates live workshops, real-time interactions, and emotionally honest moments. In the first video, he looks into the camera and says, "I love you." It's pre-recorded, but profoundly personal. No one has rejected it. "People are starving for sincerity," he says.

Building meaningful relationships in the digital age requires intentionality. It involves using digital tools to bridge gaps, create community, and facilitate spiritual growth. For the Church, this means leveraging technology to facilitate discipleship, spiritual growth, and connecting people to God and to one another.

For Kevin, it's not digital vs. physical—it's about designing for transformation. "We don't need more content," he says. "We need space—space to reflect, to be real, to meet God." And, for Terry Parkman, there is potential in seeing how the digital and physical blur. He is confident in the fact that we're going to see miracles happen in the metaverse. "What do you do when someone gets prayed for in VR and they're physically healed? Or filled with the Holy Spirit?" For Terry, this isn't hype—it's theology. The Holy Spirit is not bound by bandwidth.

LEADERS OF TOMORROW

A great asset in adapting well to what is emerging and leading into the future is embracing insights of younger individuals in our strategy and decision-making processes. The youth often spearhead innovation and swiftly adapt to cultural and technological changes. Their viewpoints can serve as invaluable compass points as we navigate these dynamic and challenging times. There have been numerous conversations with young innovative individuals with a sometimes naively positive outlook on the future that have helped shape the conversation that has resulted in this book, and it will serve you well to keep that conversation going. Rather than ditching your leadership, ignoring your experience, or just handing over responsibility to whoever's most eager, partner with and empower the younger generation to help carry forward the legacy entrusted to you. They're the ones most focused on and best suited for the future.

NOT JUST A BLIND EMBRACE OF HIGH TECH

Grasping the nuances of technology is vital. It enables global connectivity, allowing Christian education and ministry to connect with communities worldwide through online platforms, video calls, and social media. Tools like augmented and virtual reality

(VR) can deepen engagement by offering immersive, interactive learning experiences, such as virtual tours of biblical sites. Emerging technologies like AI and VR allow personalized discipleship, with content tailored to individuals and their spiritual growth. Additionally, technology increases efficiency and scalability, helping ministries automate tasks and extend their reach through online courses and digital resources.

By thoughtfully embracing these tools, ministries can adapt to modern challenges while fostering meaningful connections. While our leaders may not need to develop groundbreaking social media platforms, they should understand the implications of emerging technologies and the opportunities they present. We are traversing a continuously shifting landscape, relying on a map perpetually redrawn.

As we equip the leaders of tomorrow, we must emphasize the importance of presence and discernment alongside technological fluency. Lisa Pak's experience highlights the tension between urgency and spiritual presence, reminding us that leaders need to walk slowly enough to be interrupted, to listen, and to discern God's timing. While it's crucial for leaders to understand emerging technologies, it's equally vital for them to cultivate a Spirit-led pace that isn't dictated by a ticking clock. True leadership involves not just strategic action but also the ability to pause, recalibrate, and discern which of the "infinite possibilities" are truly for them. May your journey through this book be a moment to do just that.

A FAMILIAR CHANGE

Wimbledon. The very name evokes images of pristine green courts, strawberries and cream, and the crisp white attire of players and officials alike. For generations, a quintessential part of this tennis grand slam's allure was the familiar, authoritative voice of the line umpire—a stoic figure, hawk-eyed, with years of dedication culminating in the privilege of calling the lines, whether the ball was in or out, at the most prestigious tennis tournament in the world. Imagine the hours, the seasons spent perfecting that singular focus, the immense pressure of those championship points, all leading to that one, decisive "OUT!" or "FAULT!" that could change the course of history. To be a Wimbledon line umpire was to be part of the fabric of tennis itself, a silent guardian of fairness on hallowed ground.

But in 2025, that familiar voice, that human presence, has been subtly yet profoundly sidelined. Wimbledon, for the first time, has replaced its line umpires with an electronic line-calling system: Hawk-Eye Live.[13] Employing 18 cameras to meticulously track the ball's trajectory, the system delivers automated voice calls, triggered within a tenth of a second if a ball is deemed out. On the surface, it's a move toward enhanced accuracy and consistency, aligning with other top-level tournaments embracing similar technology. But for those who held the line, it might feel like an era has ended, replaced by a cold, calculating machine.

The transformation at Wimbledon serves as a powerful microcosm for our shifting digital existence:

Fundamentally, it underscores that digitization is neutral. The technology itself, like the

18 cameras of Hawk-Eye, is merely a tool. Its impact—whether for enhanced accuracy or the displacement of traditional roles—is determined by how it is wielded. The "ball we cannot see" is not the technology, but the neutral power it holds—and our urgent responsibility is to master the game for the sake of the cause.

Furthermore, Wimbledon's choice to use human-recorded voices for its automated calls speaks volumes about the critical need for authenticity in the digital space. Even as technology automates, our innate human need for connection and the familiar remains. This mirrors the generational shift we've discussed, where younger generations perceive digital interactions as equally authentic as physical ones, valuing transparency and consistency. For the Church, this means learning to communicate authentically in digital spaces, not shying away from vulnerability and intentionality to forge genuine connections. Perhaps the most telling detail in this technological overhaul is the deliberate choice to use human-recorded voices to deliver the calls.

So many spectators will watch, absorbed in the drama of the match, and scarcely register that a fundamental change has occurred. This echoes our innate human need for connection. As we've seen, the gospel is fundamentally about relationships—with God and one another. The digital age, with its AI companions and virtual interactions, can easily lead to a "redefinition of connectedness" where many "friends" exist online but few in real life. However, like the pandemic demonstrated, digital tools can also be lifelines, facilitating community and faith. The goal is not to digitize discipleship, but to leverage technology to create digital moments that make the next encounter more holy, fostering meaningful, authentic, and transformative experiences.

This shift at Wimbledon is not just about tennis; it's a powerful parable for the changing nature of human work and our evolving relationship with technology. The work for humans has changed, not gone away; it has simply transformed. Consider the vast ecosystem behind Hawk-Eye. How many brilliant minds at Hawk-Eye have poured countless hours into coding, engineering, and refining these complex algorithms? This is work that demands profound problem-solving, innovative design, and continuous improvement—arguably far more intellectually stimulating and fulfilling than the monotony of watching a single line while some of the most breathtaking moments in tennis history unfolds just feet away, largely unseen by the narrowly focused umpire. The digital age isn't eliminating human work entirely; it's reconfiguring it, shifting us from tasks that can be automated to roles that require uniquely human creativity, critical thinking, and complex collaboration.

In tennis, a "let" occurs when a serve touches the top of the net but still lands in the correct service box. This results in a do-over for that serve, rather than playing the point. For years at Wimbledon, this was decided by a net umpire who would hold a finger on the net to detect vibrations. This human touch was replaced in 1996, introducing a digital monitoring system with an impersonal "beep" that, for some, felt like a sterile and jarring intrusion, making the game feel less human. Yet, with Hawk-Eye, the technology is striving to be more human, not less. Technological advancement is striving to become more and more human-like. The beep, compared to the differing live-sounding shouts of fault, is telling. It is becoming increasingly difficult, and will continue to be so, to distinguish between the artificial and the human. This isn't a retreat from humanity; it's a testament to our profound need for the relatable, even as we embrace the efficiency of the digital.

This subtle yet significant evolution at Wimbledon offers a powerful glimpse into the future we are collectively stepping into. It's a future where the lines between human and digital blur, where the nature of our contributions takes new forms, and where the essence of what it means to be "human" in a technologically advanced world becomes both more complex and, paradoxically, more vital. For the Church navigating this, it's not merely an intellectual exercise; it's an imperative for fostering meaningful relationships and authentic community, ensuring we are prepared to thrive and further the gospel in an increasingly digitized world.

The rise of digital existence has brought both challenges and opportunities. On one hand, digitization risks alienating us from one another and God when it becomes a master rather than a servant. On the other hand, it offers unparalleled tools for connection, growth, and ministry when used wisely. The challenge before us is not just to exist in the digital world but to thrive in it and to further the gospel in ways that honor God and connect deeply with others.

GENUINE HUMAN INTERACTION AND UNIQUE, MEANINGFUL EXPERIENCES ARE EMERGING AS THE NEW *SCARCE RESOURCES.*

CHAPTER 4 SUMMARY

Using the story of the Marubo tribe's compressed experience with the internet, this chapter examines how digital existence is a neutral, powerful accelerant that magnifies both potential and peril. It explores three world-historic technological shifts—AI, clean energy, and bioengineering—and their impact on society. The chapter introduces the concept of the "Attention Economy" and the "Ages of Scarcity" (information, application, and now, interaction and experience), arguing that genuine human connection and meaningful experiences are becoming the new scarce resources. It challenges the Church to embrace digitization as a tool while prioritizing authenticity, real relationships, and fostering experiences that genuinely engage people, rather than getting lost in the competition for focused attention.

SKILL:

EMPLOY A HIGH-TECH & HIGH-TOUCH METHODOLOGY

REFLECTIVE QUESTIONS

1. What does "authenticity in digital spaces" look like for your leadership or ministry?

2. Are you creating and building meaningful empathetic experiences and interactions— or simply delivering more information?

3. How are you discipling others to live well in both digital and physical realities?

JOIN THE CONVERSATION
& WATCH THE INTERVIEWS HERE

PART 2

HOW THE WORLD WORKS
(STRUCTURAL)

WE ARE IN AN
'INVERSE BELL CURVE' -
A POLARIZED
REALITY WHERE THE
MIDDLE GROUND HAS
VANISHED AND
EXTREMES DOMINATE.

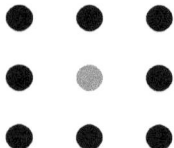

CHAPTER 5

SHIFTING DYNAMICS OF TRUST

In a world grappling with an accelerating pace of change, where even the very definition of humanity is challenged, and certainty often feels like a relic of the past, the foundations of truth and trust are shifting beneath our feet. This chapter explores how a loss of certainty in our own identities has led to a collapse of trust in the institutions that once provided stability.

THE BROKEN GLASS OF TRUST

The story of the Mona Lisa heist in 1911[1] is a powerful illustration of how trust can be both a silent guardian and a fatal weakness. For centuries, the Louvre Museum in Paris was a cathedral of art, its masterpieces protected not just by guards and walls, but by a powerful, unspoken assumption of safety. People believed that such a revered institution, the repository of humanity's greatest treasures, was untouchable. This collective trust was the invisible security system that kept the art safe.

But on August 21, 1911, an Italian handyman named Vincenzo Peruggia walked into the museum after it had closed, lifted the Mona Lisa off the wall, and simply walked out with it.[1] He wasn't a master thief; he was an employee. His success lay in exploiting a profound vulnerability: no one imagined that a museum employee, a part of the institution itself, would violate its most sacred trust. The museum, built on the assumption that its staff were trustworthy, had a massive, unseen blind spot. The trust was so deeply ingrained that it was never questioned, making it a catastrophic flaw in their security. The initial reaction wasn't even to suspect a theft, but to assume the painting had been taken for cleaning or a photograph. The assumption of trust had created a "security deficit" that, once exposed, unraveled the entire system.

This story serves as a metaphor for the shifting dynamics of trust in our own time. For centuries, institutions—whether governments, media, or the Church—have been protected by a similar invisible security system: the societal trust that they would operate with integrity and for the common good. We assumed that our leaders and organizations would uphold a shared reality and a collective set of values.

But just as Peruggia, an insider, exposed the Louvre's vulnerability, our own "insiders"— whether disillusioned individuals, fallen leaders, or the very technology that was meant to serve us—have revealed the security deficit of our institutions. The trust has been broken, and the once-impenetrable glass of our collective belief now lies in shards.

This isn't to say that all institutions are corrupt, just as the Louvre was not entirely without security, but the fundamental assumption of safety is gone. We no longer assume the glass is unbroken. Instead, we approach institutions and their messages with a baseline of suspicion. The challenge for the Church, then, is not to simply repair the glass, but to rebuild a new security system entirely, one that is not based on a fragile, unspoken assumption of trust, but on a demonstrable, consistent, and transparent commitment to truth. The "trust deficit" we face is not a technical problem; it is a human one that requires a human, and ultimately, a divine, solution.

SHIFTS:

THE SHIFT: A WORLD POLARIZED AND UNTRUSTING

For generations, we operated within a societal "bell curve," where a broad consensus anchored public discourse and credibility was largely assumed. Yet today, that familiar landscape has fractured, leaving us in an "inverse bell curve"—a polarized reality where the middle ground has vanished and extremes dominate.[2]

With her deep insight into theological training and global Christian leadership, Nicole Martin, an executive at one of the largest Christian media companies in the world, observes, "Biblically, the world is actually keeping pace with what scripture predicted. These are the last days. Darkness is rising, and principalities are pressing in." Scripture foretells the increase of division and evil, so biblically, we shouldn't be surprised by these developments. However, she warns, "The Church? The Church hasn't always kept pace with culture—and that's a problem." Just because things are bad doesn't excuse our responsibility to engage the world we were born into with the gospel.

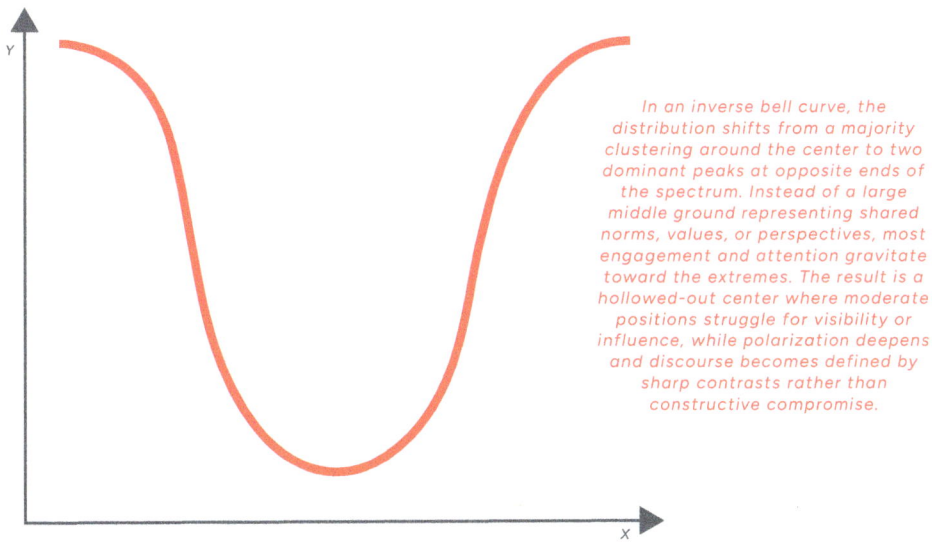

In an inverse bell curve, the distribution shifts from a majority clustering around the center to two dominant peaks at opposite ends of the spectrum. Instead of a large middle ground representing shared norms, values, or perspectives, most engagement and attention gravitate toward the extremes. The result is a hollowed-out center where moderate positions struggle for visibility or influence, while polarization deepens and discourse becomes defined by sharp contrasts rather than constructive compromise.

Figure: The Inverse Bell Curve

For generations, society largely functioned within a "bell curve" distribution. This statistical concept reflects a normal distribution where the vast majority of observations cluster around a central average, fostering a broad consensus and moderate viewpoints. Debates, though present, operated mainly from a shared understanding and common informational bedrock. However, this classic distribution has now given way to an "inverse bell curve."[2] This disquieting phenomenon describes a reality where the ideological center has collapsed, and populations have polarized toward extreme ends, leaving the middle ground virtually uninhabited.

THE CHURCH HASN'T ALWAYS KEPT PACE WITH *CULTURE*— AND THAT'S A PROBLEM.

NICOLE MARTIN

CHARACTERISTIC	BELL CURVE ERA (PRE-DIGITAL / PRE-PANDEMIC)	INVERSE CURVE ERA (DIGITAL / POST-PANDEMIC)
INFORMATION FLOW	CENTRALIZED, SHARED REALITY	FRAGMENTED, FRACTURED REALITIES
PUBLIC DISCOURSE	MODERATE CONSENSUS	POLARIZED EXTREMES
TRUST IN INSTITUTIONS	HIGH TRUST	LOW TRUST
RANGE OF OPINIONS	CLUSTERED AROUND THE MIDDLE	CLUSTERED AT OPPOSING POLES
SOCIAL COHESION	STRONG SOCIAL TIES	ERODING SOCIAL COHESION

How did we arrive at this fractured landscape? This profound societal shift is a direct consequence of the interplay between increased media choice, the subtle but powerful hand of algorithmic curation, and the unique pressures of events like the COVID-19 pandemic. In earlier eras, figures like President Franklin D. Roosevelt, through his "fireside chats," could foster national unity via centralized radio broadcasts. Similarly, trusted broadcast journalists like Walter Cronkite helped shape a collective understanding of reality for generations. These mass-market media models, despite their flaws, paradoxically created a more unified informational environment than the hyper-fragmented landscape we navigate today. Even sensationalism had a common audience, fostering a shared public conversation. The significant decline in public trust in mass media in the USA since the 1970s—from 68% in 1972 to 36% in 2024—further underscores this transition away from a shared informational reality.[3]

This polarization is deeply intertwined with a pervasive mistrust of truth and the rise of relativism. The prevailing belief has become that truth is a singular, isolated entity, discoverable only within one's own echo chamber. A fundamental aspect of this trust is what is known as "Truth Default Theory," which posits that people generally assume others are basically honest—a beneficial assumption for societal functioning—but this default is now being profoundly challenged.[4] The breakdown of trust is evident across various levels: generationally, institutionally, practically, within societal structures, and even in our own senses. This leads to instability in the fundamental trust—trust in self—and an over-reliance on charismatic communicators who emotionally connect with us, creating a false sense of safety and confidence in their message. When the subjective emotional experience of truth replaces objective evaluation, and submission to transcendent truth is abandoned, instability reigns.

Nicole highlights how the Church has contributed to this decline in trust. "In some ways," she said, "we've been like a 'hear no evil, see no evil' institution—ignoring the signs around us." She explains the "trust collapse" plainly: "We didn't pay attention to what actually builds trust in people today. It's not our branding. It's consistency. It's credibility. It's transparency." She compares the Church to Starbucks—not in theology, but in predictability. People trust Starbucks because they know what to expect, no matter the city or country. But churches? Even within the same denomination, congregations can vary dramatically. This lack of consistency leads to a loss of trust. "When we try to be everything to everyone," she says, "we end up being credible to no one."

Authenticity, transparency, and predictability, according to Nicole, are the "trust currencies of a new generation." Yet, in trying to remain "relevant," the Church often ends up undermining the very credibility people are looking for. "People want to know the truth, even when they don't agree with it," Nicole says. "But we've gotten good at polishing and performing instead of standing honestly in what we believe." She points to the lack of transparency in some churches compared to nonprofits receiving detailed financial reports from donors, noting that this lack of openness isn't just a leadership issue, but a discipleship issue. "We keep asking people to 'just trust us.' But that's not enough anymore."

Adding to the challenge, Nicole observes the dangerous effects of personal failure on public trust. "When leaders fall, especially publicly, it's not just their congregation that's impacted. There's a ripple effect. Secondary trauma. People who've never met the fallen leader walk away from Jesus because of what they saw or heard." This reality is compounded by shifts in how people consume information: "People no longer seek balanced information—they seek voices that reinforce their own." "Subscribers come and go, not based on journalistic quality, but ideological alignment." The rise of algorithm-driven news, AI-generated content, and a preference for social media for "truth" over vetted articles further exacerbates the challenge. This breakdown of trust isn't just about scandals; it's about the slow erosion of authenticity. When the community is fractured, when institutions are questioned, when no one represents the truth with humility and integrity, people stop trusting. "And when they stop trusting, they stop believing."

WHAT IF *TRUST*
IS THE APOLOGETIC
THIS GENERATION
ACTUALLY NEEDS?

LUKE GREENWOOD

IMPACT ON JESUS-FOLLOWING:

GENERATIONS DEFINED BY FOUR QUESTIONS

Without trust, the very foundation upon which a generation is built erodes. Every generation stands at a unique vantage point in history, shaped by culture, technology, and societal shifts. Yet, beneath the surface, timeless questions echo in their hearts. These are the foundational pillars upon which individuals build their lives, form their convictions, and ultimately, define their relationship with the world and with God. As we endeavor to reach and disciple the next generation, understanding and engaging with these core questions is not just helpful—it is essential. The warning from Judges 2:10—"another generation...who did not know the Lord nor the work which he had done"—serves as a stark reminder of what is at stake.

Mark Matlock introduced us to research by the Barna Group, and our conversations and engagement with younger generations confirm that their search for meaning and purpose often crystallizes around four pivotal questions.

These four fundamental questions are not unique to any single generation; rather, they are etched into the very fabric of human experience, echoing through every era, culture, and individual life. They were the core questions you grappled with as a teenager, a time of intense self-discovery and searching for your place in the world. This universal experience is why these questions also form the core themes of the movies we watch and the music we listen to. Films like Ferris Bueller's Day Off and The Breakfast Club explore the teenage quest for identity ("Who Am I?"), while Mean Girls and Stand by Me highlight the powerful need for belonging ("With Whom Do I Belong?"). Movies such as Dead Poets Society and even superhero narratives delve into what truly matters ("What Truly Matters?"), and science fiction like The Matrix or detective stories tackle the pursuit of truth ("What Is True?").

Similarly, music—from teenage anthems about identity to protest songs and ballads about belonging and values—all reflect these enduring questions. Crucially, trust is needed for all of these, and the erosion of trust in one area impacts the others:

PERSONALLY   TOGETHER

PERSONHOOD

IDENTITY
WHO AM I?

BELONGING
WITH WHO?

WORLDVIEW

VALUES
WHAT MATTERS?

EPISTEMOLOGY
WHAT IS TRUE?

1. **"Who Am I?" – The Quest for Identity:**
   At its core, this is a deep yearning for a
   stable and meaningful sense of self in an
   age of fluid identities and relentless social
   comparison. For too long, Christian
   identity has been perceived primarily
   as behavior modification. Although
   a transformed life produces changed
   behavior, an identity rooted solely in
   "do's and don'ts" remains fragile. The
   next generation seeks authenticity and an

WITHOUT *TRUST,* THE VERY *FOUNDATION* UPON WHICH A GENERATION IS BUILT *ERODES.*

   identity that resonates with their deepest being. The invitation is that Christian faith
   offers a profound answer: identity is found not in performance but in divine creation
   and gracious redemption. It's about discovering one's inherent worth as an image-
   bearer of God and understanding the new identity offered in Christ—loved, chosen,
   and called. This is an identity that is not self-constructed but received, providing a
   solid anchor. Without trust, this becomes: "I don't trust who I am."

2. **"With Whom Do I Belong?" – The Craving for Belonging:** This speaks to the
   fundamental human need for connection, acceptance, and community. In an era
   paradoxically marked by hyper-connectivity and profound loneliness, this search is
   more acute than ever. Superficial connections abound, but true belonging remains
   elusive. Young people quickly discern between performative community and genuine
   fellowship. The invitation is that the core of the Christian community is expressed in
   the simple yet profound equation: Love = Time. Meaningful belonging is cultivated
   through presence, active listening, shared experiences, and consistent investment in
   relationships. The Church is called to be an authentic community, reflecting God's
   unconditional love and offering a place where people can truly connect. Without
   trust, this manifests as: "I don't trust the places where I belong."

3. **"What Truly Matters?" – The Search for Values:** This is a generation's pursuit
   of purpose and significance. In a world offering a myriad of pursuits and causes,
   discerning lasting value from fleeting trends is a critical task. In a culture that often
   devalues commitment or presents a "cheap grace," the profound call of discipleship
   can be obscured. The invitation is that we must be willing to *restore the price to regain
   the prize.* This isn't about making faith an arduous burden to earn salvation, but about
   clearly articulating the immeasurable worth of knowing Christ and participating in
   His kingdom. For a generation wary of the superficial and hungry for a cause worthy
   of their commitment, understanding the "cost" of discipleship—the dedication,
   the surrender, the willingness to go against the grain—can actually illuminate the
   incomparable value of the "prize." This presents a vision of life rich in meaning
   because it is anchored in eternal values. Without trust, the question becomes: "I don't
   trust that what is valued is valuable."

4. **"What Is True?" – The Pursuit of Epistemology:** This reflects the innate human
   desire to understand reality and to build one's life on a solid foundation. In an
   "inverse bell curve" age of information overload, "fake news," and competing
   worldviews, navigating the path to truth is complex. Presenting faith as a closed

system of dogmatic assertions, immune to questioning, can be alienating. The invitation is to embrace the understanding that "truth is often found in the tension of debate." This doesn't mean truth itself is relative, but that the apprehension and internalization of truth often occurs through honest wrestling, open dialogue, and the freedom to explore difficult questions. Creating environments where doubts can be voiced without judgment and where intellectual engagement is encouraged builds a more resilient and deeply owned conviction. When trust is absent, this turns into: "I don't trust what I believe."

When trust crumbles, the very ground beneath a generation's feet begins to give way. Engaging these four fundamental questions is the urgent task before us. It requires us to move beyond simplistic formulas and to meet the next generation where they are, with answers that are not only biblically sound but also authentically and relationally presented. It is a call to sometimes confront the comfortable and not just comfort the conflicted—to challenge our own assumptions and methods—so that we might more effectively guide a searching generation to the One who is the ultimate answer to all their deepest questions.

SKILLS:

REBUILDING TRUST AND GUIDING TOWARD TRUTH

To address the profound impact of shifting trust dynamics, we must develop specific skills that enable us to rebuild credibility and lead people to a trustworthy God. These skills include restoring trust to the trustless, helping people understand the sources from which they derive their truth, breaking the bubbles of cultural influence, and creating psychological safety for genuine encounter.

RESTORING TRUST TO THE TRUSTLESS: THE POWER OF PRESENCE AND AUTHENTICITY

In a world where credibility has collapsed and suspicion is rampant, the first skill is to earn trust through genuine presence and authentic connection. Luke Greenwood, leading Steiger, a movement reaching Europe's post-Christian global youth culture, observes that young people aren't walking away from truth, but from trust. The Church, especially in Europe, has lost credibility—not just in its message but also in its messengers. Truth for many has been relocated from pulpits and institutions to personal experience, relationships, and community. "They're not saying truth isn't real," Luke shared. "They're saying, 'I just don't trust you to tell me what it is.'" In the U.S., deconstruction is common, but in Europe, generations never even entered a church—they're not deconstructing; they never built. Yet a hunger for truth remains; they are seekers, but they don't assume the Church is where they'll find it. The challenge isn't a lack of desire for truth, but whether they trust us enough to receive it.

Luke believes the answer lies in presence, not programs. "We can't just wait for them to come to us," he said. "We've got to go to them. And when we go, we don't start by preaching—we start by listening." This means showing up in clubs, universities, festivals, and streets—where young people actually live. Trust begins in these places, not in theological debates, but in conversation, curiosity, and community. "If people feel like you genuinely care, they're more open than you think," Luke shared. One-on-one conversations and authentic friendships often open more doors to the gospel than big events.

While digital engagement has value, Luke cautions against idolizing strategy over substance. "We think we need to be influencers," he said, "But what people really crave is community." This relational posture doesn't dilute the message; it dignifies it. Luke insists we must both build trust and speak truth, as truth can only be heard when trust is present. He recounts his band's outreach in a secular club in Warsaw, where building trust within the music community allowed them to talk about Jesus from the stage, and people listened out of respect for authenticity and genuine care.

Luke sees this as a model: be salt and light. Salt is distinct and preserves; light is visible and shines. But if we're only salty, people won't come near. If we're only light, we might lose clarity. The power is in being both—distinct and present, clear and compassionate. Leaders must shift from boardroom planning to starting on the ground: "Walk among people first. Learn their culture, their values, and their fears. Then your message will actually connect." This all flows from a deep relationship with Jesus. "If I'm rooted in Him," Luke said, "I don't go to the world to be influenced. I go to influence. I go to love." His team's first value is simple: seek God. Love must precede mission. If we truly love, we'll listen, go to them, build trust, and then speak truth in love—with clarity, not compromise. In a world that no longer trusts institutions but longs for truth, the Church's invitation is: Show up. Listen well. Love deeply. Speak clearly. Be present.

> THEY'RE NOT SAYING
> TRUTH ISN'T REAL,
> THEY'RE SAYING,
> 'I JUST DON'T *TRUST*
> YOU TO TELL ME
> WHAT IT IS.'
> **LUKE GREENWOOD**

Jiyoung Yoo, a fourth-generation Korean Christian leader, publisher, connector, and influencer, emphasizes that understanding the future of truth and trust requires understanding the present crisis. She describes a profound fracture: "It's not that truth itself is changing; it's that our interactions with people and information have lost the traditional trust that once held them together." In the social media age, trust is shallow and transactional. People consume online content not from deep belief, but for momentary benefit, like entertainment or information. "We don't really trust influencers," Jiyoung explained. "We accept what they give us because it serves us. And when they fall, we move on without emotional damage—because there was never real trust to begin with." This shallowness stems from exhaustion, as her generation has witnessed countless betrayals. "We're not choosing not to trust out of rebellion," she said. "We're afraid. Our society runs on fear." Unchecked fear fuels polarization, becoming a weapon groups use to gain power.

Jiyoung points to a different fuel: trust in God. In a society saturated with distrust, the antidote isn't merely trusting people more, but deepening our trust in God and living out His love toward others. "God never asked us to protect Him or protect the Church," she said. "He asked us to trust Him—and love people." This trust is born from relationship: "You can't trust God if you don't know Him." Trust grows through exposure, experience, and shared life. "The more you know God, the more you realize you can't not trust Him." This also applies to people: authentic love precedes trust. "We're not called to trust people immediately—we're called to love them; and as we love and know them, trust naturally grows."

Jiyoung's observations reveal the devastating consequences of a society stripped of deep trust. Without real relationships and commitment, even our belief in truth crumbles. In a world where complexity outstrips comprehension, people struggle to find foundations, not knowing which voices to believe. Yet, Jiyoung's hope is clear: authenticity still shines, and true transparency is deeply attractive. However, transparency isn't the goal; obedience to God is, and real obedience requires real transparency. Leading in such a world demands deep integrity: *what you say must align with what you live.* The temptation to sell ideas without embodying them must be resisted, as only what is truly authentic will last. Jiyoung challenges the Church to rethink its relationship with science and discovery. Historically, Christians have feared new knowledge, but true discovery only reveals more of God's complexity. "And that should comfort us. His mystery is part of His greatness." Rather than fear, the Church must lead with courage, welcoming new knowledge to deepen awe, not diminish faith. Ultimately, Jiyoung believes the next chapter of the Church and faith is "hope."

LEARNING TO TRUST TRUTH: THE EGGBERT ANALOGY

To help people navigate this fractured landscape and rebuild their capacity to trust truth, we must equip them to understand their own sources of truth, particularly when their minds get in the way of belief in Jesus. The notion of believing and thinking simultaneously might seem paradoxical to some, especially in an era marked by deep mistrust. We often encounter unanswered questions, aspects of faith that stretch beyond our immediate grasp. Yet, the presence of mystery doesn't inherently negate the logical coherence of Jesus' teachings. The key lies in understanding the logic behind faith—how we can engage with, live in, and ultimately be grounded in truth—a journey that is fundamentally about learning to trust what is truly real.

To illustrate this, let's consider the predicament of Eggbert the Egg. Eggbert was an average egg in every way, yet he struggled with the concept of gravity. He knew other eggs who attended the "Heavy Church" and believed in gravity, but for Eggbert, the idea of an invisible, mysterious force pulling everything downwards just didn't resonate.

Why did Eggbert struggle to believe in gravity? And, by extension, why do we sometimes struggle to believe in what we believe? The answer often lies in our epistemology – our theory of knowledge, the methods and validity of our beliefs. Historically, four major schools of thought have prevailed in defining truth:

1. **Consensus (It Is True Because We Agree):** This perspective suggests that truth is what has been intellectually agreed upon over the ages; the idea being, "They cannot all be wrong." Trust in this system is placed in the collective wisdom and established authority. If Eggbert subscribed to this, gravity would be true because everyone around him agreed

it was, and he would trust that collective agreement as the basis for his belief.

2. **Practical (It Works):** Rooted in the scientific model, this view holds that truth is tried, tested, experimented with, and proven to be factual. Life is approached as one big experiment. Trust here is built on verifiable results and repeatable experiences. For Eggbert, if gravity could be demonstrated and consistently produce the same results, he might accept it, placing his trust in the tangible evidence.

3. **Relative (It Depends):** In this post-truth era, truth is often seen as subjective to each individual; it's not whether it's true, but whether it's true for you. This approach fundamentally erodes shared trust, as individual feelings become the ultimate arbiter of reality, making genuine consensus impossible. If Eggbert held this view, gravity would only be true if it felt true to him in that moment, meaning his trust would be entirely self-referential and highly unstable.

4. **True in Itself (A Priori):** This school of thought posits that truth is an entity beyond perception, something to be discovered rather than developed. Truth, in essence, defends itself. Learning to trust this inherent, transcendent truth is the foundational step toward a stable belief system, regardless of personal feelings or popular opinion. For Eggbert, gravity would simply be a fundamental, undeniable aspect of reality, regardless of his belief—a truth he would ultimately need to trust, even if he didn't fully comprehend it.

Who we find trust in and how we define truth have profound consequences. Eggbert didn't believe in gravity, and he was content in his disbelief, yet he always wondered about that persistent pulling sensation. Ultimately, Eggbert fell.

Our beliefs are directly connected to what we hold as true, and what is true is worthy of our belief. If God is true, then His truth should impact every facet of our lives. Yet, many of us live in a "twilight zone" between genuine belief and apathetic indifference. Jesus faced similar challenges during His earthly ministry; not everyone accepted what He shared as truth. He told the parable of the sower in Luke 8. The seed, Jesus explained, is the word of God, distributed as principles to live by. Different people responded in different ways: On the Path (Consensus), Amongst the Thorns (Practical), and The Shallow Ground (Relative). However, the parable doesn't end there. There is also the Good Soil (True in Itself). These are those with noble and good hearts, who hear the word, retain it, and persevere to produce a crop. If truth is a seed, then the act of trusting that seed, receiving it, and nurturing it in the depths of your heart is essential for it to bear fruit. It must be allowed to have an effect on you, changing you from the inside out. You cannot truly know God objectively, just as you cannot build a relationship objectively. Instead, we must make the conscious choice to trust God by allowing Him in, allowing the seed of truth to grow and develop in our hearts. As John 3:8 states, "The wind blows wherever it pleases. You hear its sound, but you cannot tell where it comes from or where it is going. So it is with everyone born of the Spirit." Like the wind through the trees, allow Him to blow over your life. Risk making yourself subject to Him, receive His word, and plant it deep within your heart.

The effects of this "wind" on our understanding of truth become clear. First, the Bible holds immense consensus—being the most read, printed, replicated online, and installed app in history. Second, the practical and transformative power of Jesus' truth has proven supremely valuable for every aspect of life, standing the test of time. And third, as Eggbert discovered, the stark reality is that relativism yields no good fruit, producing nothing substantial in life. However, within the understanding of truth being true in itself, every other level of understanding becomes a valuable tool for finding the Truth. This foundational trust in a truth beyond ourselves is what truly empowers us. Ultimately, the choice to believe and to trust in this transcendent reality is ours. God is not far from any of us. He is as true as gravity. Don't be an Eggbert; instead, choose to trust the ultimate reality and fall into the arms of God. Acts 17 reminds us that God made everything—gravity, wind, and even eggs—so that we might seek Him and find Him, for He is not far from any of us.

BURSTING THE CULTURE BUBBLE: A FOUNDATION FOR TRUST

To truly embrace truth and foster trust in the gospel, we must help people recognize and break free from the "belief bubbles" that distort their understanding. Culture can be vividly described as the invisible "pattern" or "mold" within which we live our lives. Every person exists within their own unique cultural bubble, shaped by their upbringing, environment, social circles, and the media they consume. These bubbles become problematic when we mistake the limited perspectives within them for the entirety of truth. The critical question for us is: "Are you living in a bubble, or are you truly living in the truth?"

To break free, we must actively seek to burst these personal and communal bubbles. This journey involves a willingness to confront our own biases and discomforts:

• **Be Unpopular (Deal with Peer Pressure):** Our beliefs are often shaped by those around us. True freedom and genuine belief come from grounding our identity and convictions in our relationship with God, rather than in the shifting sands of peer opinion.

• **Be Humble (History & Habits):** Our personal histories, deeply ingrained habits, and past experiences form a powerful filter through which we perceive the world. A vital lesson in living outside the bubble is recognizing that "your perspective is not always true."

• **Be Uncomfortable (Embrace the Road of Resistance):** Life often nudges us toward the "road of least resistance." Breaking free means choosing the harder, more resistant road when it aligns with God's will, demonstrating a conviction that can inspire trust.

The comforting illusion of a bubble cannot last forever. Eventually, every bubble bursts. Recognizing that our perception and understanding of truth is limited, even though God's truth is infinite, goes a long way toward building trust.

CREATING PSYCHOLOGICAL SAFETY TO HELP US MEET IN THE MIDDLE

The anxiety experienced in the world today is often a result of a lack of trust coupled with high expectations of performance. To restore trust, we must embrace the process of establishing trust before presenting truth. This means inviting people through a door, not confronting them with a brick wall. It calls for a discovery-centric theology, rather than one solely focused on definitions, fostering an experience of God. We must embrace the discovery of truth in the tension of debate, cultivating an environment of psychological safety.

HOW PSYCHOLOGICAL SAFETY
RELATES TO PERFORMANCE STANDARDS

	PSYCHOLOGICAL SAFETY — LOW ↕ HIGH	
	COMFORT ZONE **FRIENDLY, BUT FLAT** Nice vibes, no breakthroughs Conversations stay safe Growth stalls	**LEARNING ZONE** **HIGH TRUST, HIGH GROWTH** Curiosity drives performance Smart risks, bold ideas Innovation happens here
	APATHY ZONE **CHECKED IN, TUNED OUT** Present, not engaged Energy + creativity missing Performance erodes	**ANXIETY ZONE** **FEAR AT THE WHEEL** Voices go silent Ideas supressed Work + team at risk

LOW ← **PERFORMANCE STANDARDS** → HIGH

See Business Infographics. (2024, March 7). *How psychological safety is related to performance [Infographic]*. LinkedIn. https://www.linkedin.com/posts/business-infographics_how-psychological-safety-related-to-performance-activity-7157492539824979968-sWCU

Psychological safety, as Amy Edmondson's model illustrates, is the foundation for a "learning zone" where people can collaborate and learn in the service of high performance without fear of offering new ideas or asking for help.[5] This is the ideal environment for the Church to operate in—moving people out of the "anxiety zone" (low psychological safety, high performance standards) where they are reluctant to offer ideas, and the "apathy zone" (low psychological safety, low performance standards) where they choose self-protection over exertion. When the Church provides a psychologically safe space, people are willing to be vulnerable, ask difficult questions, and wrestle with doubt, which is the fertile ground where trust is rebuilt.

Terry Parkman therefore draws our attention to what the world today desires most: stability. "Trust is found in what is consistent. Pure. Whole. Just." That's why, even in a digital age, people aren't just looking for information—they're craving embodiment. "We embody trust the way devices embody simplicity. We become the thing that offers peace in the chaos."

Ultimately, the mission is unmistakable: to accelerate Christianity into the future, we must address the profound shifts in trust that define our time. As the insights from Luke Greenwood, Jiyoung Yoo, and Nicole Martin underscore, "Trust is no longer built by titles. It's built by time and presence." This generation is not allergic to truth, but suspicious of anyone claiming to own it. "What if trust is the apologetic this generation actually needs?" We must lead people back toward trust—not by demanding it, but by earning it.

THE TRUTH IS *INFALLIBLE,* BUT WE AREN'T, AND OUR CREDIBILITY GROWS WHEN WE'RE WILLING TO SAY, 'I GOT THAT WRONG.'
NICOLE MARTIN

THERE IS HOPE

Moving Christianity forward requires confronting the significant shifts in trust that are shaping our era. This involves understanding the polarized society we inhabit and the deep mistrust of truth that has taken root. By recognizing the four foundational questions defining this generation—identity, belonging, values, and truth itself—we can see how the erosion of trust undermines the very fabric of their lives.

Our response must be rooted in intentional skills. We must empower people to discern truth by helping them understand the sources of their beliefs, breaking them free from cultural bubbles that obscure reality. Crucially, we must cultivate psychological safety, embracing a discovery-centric approach that fosters genuine encounters with God's truth in the tension of debate. As we've been reminded: we've been trying to preach clarity into a fog. But what if the clarity they need isn't about facts—it's about knowing we care? In a world of "fishbowls and avatars" where we are exposed yet often pretending, it's no wonder trust is eroding. The gospel doesn't start with trust in people. It starts with trust in God. We've taught performance but forgotten presence, leading to curated loneliness. Transparency isn't the goal. Obedience is. But real obedience will always require real transparency. People want answers, but perhaps what they truly need is safety, and when the Church provides that, trust will be rebuilt.

Nicole Martin's final thoughts resonate: "The truth is infallible. But we aren't. And our credibility grows when we're willing to say, 'I got that wrong.'" The Church's future depends on cultivating trust through consistent presence and humility, showing a generation what genuine faithfulness looks like. This is about rebuilding trust, not with perfect people, but with transparent, humble lives that point beyond themselves to a trustworthy Savior. "We're not looking for the next big idea—we're looking for the ancient anchor. And when everything else moves, that's where we plant ourselves." Let that be what's next.

Ultimately, for Jiyoung, the next chapter of the Church and of faith is summarized in one word: hope. "We already know the end," she said with a smile. "Hope is always what's next." In a world where truth is fragile, trust is fractured, and fear threatens to reign, our hope in God—anchored in deep relationship, radical authenticity, and courageous love—remains unshakable.

CHAPTER 5 SUMMARY

This chapter diagnoses a societal shift from a "bell curve" of shared consensus to an "inverse bell curve" of extreme polarization and pervasive mistrust. It argues that this collapse of trust results from fragmented information, a rise in relativism, and a lack of consistency and transparency from institutions, including the Church. The chapter frames the current generation's search for meaning around four core questions: Who am I? With whom do I belong? What truly matters? And what is true?. It proposes that the Church must rebuild trust not by demanding it but by earning it through genuine presence, vulnerability, and a willingness to admit fault. Leaders are challenged to move beyond "bubbles" of cultural conformity and create psychologically safe environments where people can discover truth in the tension of debate.

SKILL:

EMBRACE THE PROCESS OF ESTABLISHING TRUST BEFORE PRESENTING TRUTH

REFLECTIVE QUESTIONS

1. In your context, what are the key reasons people no longer trust the Church or its leaders?

2. How can you build trust in a polarized world without compromising truth?

3. What would it mean to stop "protecting" the Church's image and start rebuilding its credibility?

JOIN THE CONVERSATION
& WATCH THE INTERVIEWS HERE

A *LEADER* OF THE
FUTURE IS THE
ONE WHO DOESN'T
NEED TO BE *SEEN*.

JENN BROWN

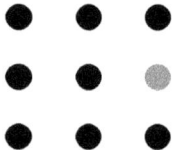

CHAPTER 6

SHIFTING DIMENSIONS OF ORGANIZATION

This breakdown of trust, combined with the accelerating pace of technology, is causing old organizational structures to unravel. This chapter explores how institutions—from global companies to local churches—are being forced to re-evaluate how they are structured and led in a world of fractured realities and eroding trust.

The world isn't just changing; its fundamental dimensions are shifting. The forces that once pulled us together are now pushing us apart, creating new divides and exacerbating old ones. Understanding this great unraveling—the increasing concentration of wealth, the widening technological chasm, the reversal brought by automation, and the growing self-sufficiency of individuals and nations—is crucial. Just as a map becomes useless when the terrain it depicts radically alters, our old models of understanding the world may no longer serve us. This echoes the predicament described by Tod Bolsinger in "Canoeing the Mountains,"[1] where Lewis and Clark, equipped for river travel, suddenly found themselves confronted with vast mountain ranges they were unprepared for. Their existing tools and maps were rendered obsolete by the new terrain. Similarly, the Church today faces its own "mountains"—a dramatically fragmented and complex landscape for which our traditional "canoes" of ministry and organization are ill-equipped. The question now is, what new maps will we draw to navigate this increasingly fragmented and complex landscape and effectively hit the ball we cannot yet see?

In the late 1990s, Blockbuster Video stood as an undisputed entertainment industry titan. With over 9,000 stores globally, it was the quintessential "results economy" success story: tangible assets, predictable revenue from rentals and late fees, and a physical footprint that seemed invincible.[2] Families flocked to its brightly lit aisles on Friday nights, browsing shelves filled with the latest releases, making it a beloved weekend ritual. Renting a video and later a DVD to take home to view was solid business. Blockbuster wasn't just a business; it was a cultural institution, a seemingly unshakable empire built on a clear, established model of entertainment delivery.

Yet, lurking in the shadows was a small, ambitious company called Netflix. Founded in 1997, Netflix initially operated as a DVD-by-mail service.[3] Its value proposition was different: no late fees, a subscription model, and direct delivery to your home. On the surface, it seemed a minor inconvenience to the Blockbuster behemoth. Blockbuster even had the chance to buy Netflix for a paltry $50 million in 2000 but famously declined, viewing it as a niche service with no real threat to their established model.[3]

They were hitting the ball they could see, perfectly within the lines of their established game.

JUST AS A MAP BECOMES USELESS WHEN THE TERRAIN IT DEPICTS RADICALLY *ALTERS*, OUR OLD MODELS OF UNDERSTANDING THE WORLD MAY NO LONGER *SERVE* US.

The unraveling, however, was already in motion. What Blockbuster failed to see was that the game itself was changing. The internet was rapidly transforming not just how information was accessed, but how attention was captured and how value was delivered. Netflix wasn't just mailing DVDs; it was gathering data, refining algorithms, and building a foundation for a future where content would be streamed directly into homes, eliminating physical stores entirely. Blockbuster was trapped by its successful past, unable to adapt its "maps" to the invisible, rapidly shifting terrain of the digital age. This dramatic shift, where a seemingly invincible empire crumbled because it failed to recognize the new currency of attention and the power of digital delivery, serves as a powerful cautionary tale for any institution, including the Church, navigating the turbulent waters of the 21st century.

The way we consume things changes; if companies miss it, they disappear. But how are these changes in the way the world works impacting the Church and global missions? It starts on the personal level and then escalates to companies, community, government, and the globe. This chapter explores the shift that is taking place in the way humans organize at every level, as the shifts explored in the previous chapters, changing the human experience, start playing out in organizations and global economic and political arenas.

For decades, the global narrative seemed clear: increasing connectedness made the world feel as if it were shrinking. The rise of the G8 and G20, the expansion of the European Union, and the digital networks forged by the internet all pointed to a future of increasing integration and collaboration. We celebrated a flattening world, where geographical boundaries blurred and shared interests seemed to outweigh nationalistic impulses. January 2020 marked the realization of BREXIT, with the United Kingdom leaving the European Union after half a century, a jarring signal that perhaps the tide was turning. Now, as borders firm up and nationalistic movements surge, it's becoming starkly apparent that the dimensions of our organizations, governments, and even our most fundamental relationships are undergoing a profound and often paradoxical shift.

Global structures, along with the framework of companies and organizations are unraveling in unpredictable and complex ways. What is clear is that as the human experience is changing, waves of reaction and counterreaction are rippling through society's structures. Learning to respond accurately to these shifts is essential as we build our own frameworks, engage with global structures, and are shaped by them—all while seeking to reach every person on the planet with the gospel.

In his time, the prominent German Lutheran pastor and neo-orthodox theologian, Dietrich Bonhoeffer, keenly observed the deepening divisions and polarization within Germany that would ultimately lead to World War II. He had a unique clarity in recognizing how easily people could be swayed by ideologies that prioritized opposition and defined identity by "what one is 'against.'" Bonhoeffer's writings powerfully underscore the profound dangers of such societal fragmentation, highlighting how seemingly innocuous disagreements could escalate into fierce ideological battles, ultimately paving the way for the atrocities that followed. His experience reveals a profound connection between an identity defined by opposition and the escalation of conflict, providing an urgent warning for the contemporary Church.

This historical predicament offers a powerful parallel to the challenges facing the global Church today. Bonhoeffer's era of profound societal fragmentation, with its escalating polarization and the breakdown of shared reality, echoes our own "great unraveling." In the face of these divisive forces, the established German churches largely chose a path of compromise and complicity, prioritizing their own institutional survival over their moral and prophetic duty. This is a stark warning for the Church today, which, in a similar context of ideological conformity and division, risks becoming "repulsive to society" by losing its individual conscience and prophetic voice.

Yet, Bonhoeffer's life and theology offer a profound and hopeful counter-narrative. "Silence in the face of evil is itself evil: God will not hold us guiltless. Not to speak is to speak. Not to act is to act."[4] This call to moral courage and unity in the face of division is precisely the response needed today. Bonhoeffer's enduring legacy is a powerful reminder that our mission is not to seek comfort or institutional self-preservation, but to courageously and sacrificially live out a faith that exists for the sake of the world.

This leads us to examine the key shifts that are reshaping the dimensions of organizations and demanding a new approach to faith in the future.

SHIFTS:

Having laid out the macro shifts impacting the world and the cautionary tale of Blockbuster, we now turn our attention to the specific ways these forces are reshaping how humans organize at every level. The fragmentation we've observed isn't just an abstract concept; it's playing out in tangible shifts within our societal structures, from individual relationships to global economics and politics. Understanding these changes is critical for the Church, as it seeks to navigate an increasingly complex landscape and effectively communicate the gospel locally and to the farthest corners of the world.

One of the most profound shifts underway is the rise of self-sufficiency, coupled with ever-widening chasms across various dimensions of human experience. These two forces—a growing tendency toward individual and national independence, and the increasing disparities in wealth, technology, and access—are fundamentally altering the fabric of our communities and global interactions.

THE WIDENING CHASM: WEALTH AND TECHNOLOGY

The most visible manifestation of this unraveling is the widening wealth divide. A handful of individuals now control more wealth than the bottom half of the global population, fundamentally reshaping power dynamics and influencing political agendas and access to opportunities. This economic chasm is inextricably linked to the technological divide. While digital tools promised democratization, they've also created new fault lines, where those with access to advanced technology and digital literacy surge ahead, leaving others marginalized.

These divides create a relevance deficit for the Church. If we don't understand and engage with these disparities, we risk becoming stagnant and losing ground, especially among generations excluded from digital participation. Leaders must grasp this, as traditional ministry "canoes" are ill-equipped for this fragmented landscape. The Church is called to bridge these gaps, living out the gospel in contexts of extreme inequality and digital exclusion. The top 1% of the global population earns almost half of the world's wealth, and owning a car places an individual within the top 10% of wealthiest people worldwide.[5] This stark divide between rich and poor is further intensified by the ultra-rich—the top 0.001%— who not only control disproportionate amounts of wealth but also wield influence as celebrities and politicians, effectively shaping public opinion and amplifying their beliefs over traditional ones. Wisely responding to this, while elevating the voice of the marginalized, will determine the credibility of our gospel presentation.

THE STORY OF THE SHOE: WHEN A ROBOT REPLACED A VILLAGE

For decades, the story of the running shoe was a story of globalization. It was a tale of threads and rubber, of designs born in corporate headquarters in the West, and of a manufacturing journey that spanned thousands of miles to a factory floor in a developing nation. The journey was dictated by a single, unshakable economic principle: the pursuit of cheaper labor. This dynamic created an entire ecosystem of prosperity. A company like Adidas could dramatically reduce its production costs, and in turn, a village in Vietnam, or a small city in Indonesia, could build an economy. Young women and men would leave their rural homes for the city, finding steady, even if demanding, work. The factories became the new town square, and a burgeoning middle class emerged, fueled by a global demand for affordable sneakers. The system was, in its own way, a kind of global partnership, a fragile but powerful engine of economic parity built on the back of manual labor.

Then, the game changed.

The change wasn't announced with a fanfare or a public declaration of a new economic philosophy. It was quietly unveiled in a nondescript building in Ansbach, Germany, in 2015. It was the first Adidas Speedfactory.[6] This was not just a new factory; it was a glimpse into a new world. The factory floor was eerily quiet, a stark contrast to the buzzing, densely populated plants of Southeast Asia. Here, the work was done not by human hands, but by robots. A complex, automated assembly line, guided by intelligent software and precision machinery, could produce a running shoe from start to finish with minimal human intervention. The need to send designs across the globe was gone. The logistical complexity of managing a far-flung supply chain was drastically reduced. The very thing that had anchored a global industry—the need for cheap human labor—was becoming obsolete.

The implications of this shift are staggering. The Speedfactory could churn out 500,000 pairs of shoes a year,[7] but more importantly, it could do so near the consumer markets of Europe and North America, reducing shipping costs and improving response times. The "why" of the factory was no longer "to find cheap labor," but "to be fast and close." The story of the shoe was no longer a journey of globalization; it was a journey of automation and localization.

This offers a vivid parable for the "Automation Reversal" we are living through. For decades, the flow of capital and jobs moved from the developed world to the developing world, creating a fragile but real economic interdependence. The allure of cheap labor was the primary gravitational force. But as robotics and AI become more sophisticated and cost-effective, that force is losing its power. The Speedfactory model is now being replicated by other industries, threatening to undo the economic gains of many developing nations. The work of the world is no longer being done by human hands alone; it is being done by machines, and those machines can be placed anywhere. The economic parity that was created by the global pursuit of cheap labor is being reversed, creating new challenges for global missions and community development. The question for the Church is not just how to reach people in these changing contexts, but how to minister to communities whose economic foundations are literally being automated out of existence.

This reversal is one of the key shifts challenging traditional models of organization and ministry, much like Blockbuster's failure to see the changing landscape of media consumption. The Church must now, more than ever, develop new "maps" and "canoes" to navigate this new terrain. Our old approaches, which may have worked in a world where economic engagement was a clear path to mission, may no longer serve us. We must learn to respond with wisdom, creativity, and a deep sense of purpose to a world where the dimensions of our organizations are shifting in ways we have not yet fully comprehended.

This change risks reversing economic progress in many developing nations, potentially exacerbating wealth divides. This economic restructuring impacts global missions and development efforts. How should the Church adapt its approaches to sustainable ministry and community development in regions that may face renewed economic hardship due to automation, especially since evangelism and social good were once linked to industrial expansion in developing nations?

THE SELF-SUFFICIENT MICROCOSM FROM INDIVIDUALS TO NATIONS

Perhaps the most insidious shift is increasing self-sufficiency at both individual and national levels. We now meet almost every need virtually, from shopping to social interaction, chipping away at local communities, and the necessity of real-world relationships. This individual self-sufficiency is mirrored by the resurgence of national self-sufficiency. Nationalistic movements prioritize domestic interests, closing borders and restricting international engagement, often framed around security and economic resilience. This counteracts global interconnectedness, risking trade wars, stifled innovation, and a diminished capacity to address global challenges. This shift amplifies polarization, as individuals increasingly gravitate toward news sources and social circles that reinforce their existing views, leading to a breakdown in shared reality and pushing society toward ideological extremes, driven by algorithms that prioritize content aligned with specific cultural identities. In an alarming global trend, India, mirroring the trajectory of certain Islamic nations, is demonstrating an intensifying aspiration to redefine itself as a Hindu nation. This overt and increasingly assertive shift toward a polarized identity, moving decisively away from any pretense of moderation, is directly correlated with a disturbing surge in religious persecution. The very fabric of societal harmony and global understanding appears to be unraveling, as the world seems to have forfeited its capacity for empathetic listening and genuine mutual comprehension.

IF OUR GOAL IS TO *REACH EVERYONE*, THEN WE HAVE TO FACE THE INCONVENIENT TRUTH THAT LIFE IS ABOUT TO GET MUCH *HARDER* AND MUCH *DIFFERENT* FOR MANY WHOM GOD LOVES AS MUCH AS HE LOVES THE FEW WHO HAVE THE MOST.

As the dimensions of human organization shift toward greater self-sufficiency and the chasms between us widen, the challenge of effectively engaging with the future of faith becomes more complex. How can we hope to hit a ball that is increasingly out of reach for many, obscured by the very disparities that are reshaping our world? The expanding divide doesn't just represent a physical or technological distance; it signifies a growing rift in perspective, experience, and access to the very resources needed to navigate this new terrain. To accelerate Christianity into the future, we must not only learn to see the ball despite the fog of change, but also find ways to bridge these chasms so that all are empowered to step up to the plate.

If our goal is simply to reach some—those who are like us, living with similar resources and access—we can brush these dynamics aside as only somewhat relevant to us. But if our goal is to reach everyone, we must confront the inconvenient truth: life is about to become far more difficult and drastically different as we seek to reach the many whom God loves just as much as the few who have the most.

IMPACT ON JESUS-FOLLOWING:

In an increasingly divided world, the Church stands at a critical juncture, faced with the profound choice of whether to become a further fragmenting force or a beacon of unity. The very forces of self-sufficiency and widening chasms that define our age—from technological disparities to economic inequalities—are reshaping not only society but also how the global Church positions itself. To truly "hit the ball we cannot see," we must move beyond traditional approaches, embracing creativity and invention to bridge the growing divides. This means actively connecting the "haves" and "have-nots," empowering individuals with a broader worldview, and redoubling our efforts to uplift the disempowered. The industrial and geopolitical shifts unfolding around us have the power to either stifle or significantly advance the cause of a truly counter-cultural Church, and our response to these seismic changes will ultimately determine our impact on the future of faith.

A CHURCH DISCONNECTED FROM ITS MISSION

The challenges of a polarized and self-sufficient world have profoundly impacted the Church's ability to fulfill its mission, leading it to become increasingly disconnected from its original purpose of existing for others. The danger is that Christianity will be seen as either the majority and become the oppressor of minorities, being rejected by the next generation, or become the minority and face persecution. The consumer-driven mindset has led to a retreat from this missional purpose, transforming the Church into a place of comfort and passive observation. Vince Parker, a key next-gen leader from Life.Church, shares, "Many in the older generation still treat church like a restaurant—show up, get fed, and leave. But the younger generation sees the church more like home. 'We've got work to do here,' they say." This is a direct consequence of shifts in individual self-sufficiency and the digital landscape, where passive consumption no longer suffices.

THE NEED FOR A NEW LEADERSHIP MODEL

Kristen Shuler, who leads East-West's global operations, offers a clear conviction: the mission hasn't changed—but how we live it out must. She sees the old model of sending missionaries from the West to the rest rapidly fading as the primary missions strategy. "The most effective strategy now is equipping local leaders." This groundswell of indigenous believers is already passionate and active, so much so that "We're not casting the vision," she says, "We're catching up to it." This shift isn't just strategic—it's spiritual. It demands humility, requiring organizations rooted in tradition to lay down old mindsets and the idea that "we are the solution." "We're not the saviors of the world. Jesus is. Our job is to fan the flame that's already burning in local churches around the globe."

Kristen also challenges the Church's approach to generosity, noting that it often taps into ego, but true generosity mirrors the heart of the Father and is an act of worship, a way to partner with what God is already doing in hidden corners of the world. She points to the courage of believers in India, facing life imprisonment for "conversion," who are gathering to pray for their persecutors in prison. Kristen calls this rising generation a prophetic voice in a polarized world because their identity in Christ is so rooted that they are willing to lose everything. "The vision is there," she says. "Our role is to resource it—whether through finances, training, Scripture access, or mentorship."

SKILLS:

To combat the pervasive polarization and organizational shifts of our age, the Church must develop specific skills that move people from isolated existence to collaborative participation. This requires building transformational communities and fostering a new kind of leadership that prioritizes serving over being served. We must break the transactional loop that has led to a consumerist mindset and instead embrace a transformational loop where changed people change people and society.

These shifts are a combination of adjustments in the way we engage the world as it reorganizes, and also how we need to reorganize the organizations where we lead.

HOLDING TRUTH IN TENSION

Truth is often held in tension, much like the forces that hold up a bridge. Concepts such as truth and grace, judgment and mercy, and love and holiness reveal God in their complexity and relationship with one another. Our polarized society often presents a single truth as the singular truth, but all truth is held in the tension of two extremes. Developing the ability to present truth within that framework enables us to reconnect people in the middle and create common ground amidst societal polarization.

We instinctively view tension as a problem to be solved. It's the uncomfortable friction in a relationship, the painful throbbing of a toothache, the dissonant note in a melody. Our impulse is to eliminate it, to find the quickest path back to harmony and ease. But what if we've fundamentally misread the nature of tension? Consider the Golden Gate Bridge. It is not a monument to the absence of tension, but to its perfect, beautiful management. Two immense cables, each composed of 27,572 individual wires, are stretched between two towers, bearing the weight of the roadway below. They are in a constant state of extreme tension, pulling against the towers which are, in turn, anchored deep into the earth. It is not the *lack* of tension that allows thousands of cars to cross safely every day; it is the tension itself, meticulously balanced and harnessed. To "solve" the tension in the Golden Gate Bridge would be to sever its cables, instantly collapsing the entire structure into the bay.

This is the kind of tension the Church is called to manage in a polarized world. It is not the unhealthy tension of conflict that must be resolved, but the load-bearing tension of theological paradoxes and complex truths. We are called to be like the engineers of that great bridge, not severing the cables of grace to satisfy the demands of law, or cutting the anchor of holiness to make love more palatable. Instead, our task is to hold these truths in their beautiful, powerful, and necessary opposition. By doing so, we create a structure of faith that is not only strong enough to bear the weight of a complex world but also provides a pathway for people to cross from the shores of division and distrust to a place of genuine, resilient community. We become a people who can manage the tension, not by resolving it, but by trusting the design.

BUILDING A TEAM OF TEAMS

General Stanley McChrystal wasn't a man given to nostalgia. He was a creature of precision, of data, of the cold calculus of war. But in the mid-2000s, as he led the Joint Special Operations Task Force in Iraq, he found himself trapped in a new kind of war, one where the enemy didn't play by the old rules. Al-Qaeda in Iraq (AQI) was a hydra-headed beast, decentralized and adaptive. McChrystal's team was a finely tuned machine, a collection of elite units like the Navy SEALs and Delta Force, but they were a machine built for a different era. They were a "Team of Experts," a collection of specialists who worked in silos, each unit executing its mission with unparalleled efficiency, but rarely collaborating.[8]

The problem wasn't a lack of talent; it was a lack of speed. While McChrystal's team was planning a raid, AQI was already adapting, changing tactics, and disappearing into the civilian population.[8] A raid planned in the morning might be obsolete by the afternoon. The intelligence gathering, analysis, and action cycle was too slow. It was a classic case of an industrial-age organization facing an information-age threat. McChrystal realized they were losing not because they were less skilled, but because they were less connected. The enemy was a network, and his team was a hierarchy.[8]

McChrystal's solution was radical, almost heretical. He broke down the walls between his elite units. He forced them to share information, to collaborate, and to build relationships. He embedded a Navy SEAL with an Army Ranger unit, a Delta Force operator with a CIA analyst. He created a "shared consciousness" where everyone, from the lowest-ranking soldier to the commanding general, had a common understanding of the battlefield. This wasn't just about sharing data; it was about building trust and empathy. He transformed his "Team of Experts" into a "Team of Teams" where the whole was greater than the sum of its parts. This new approach, born out of necessity and a near-constant state of failure, became the guiding principle that allowed them to finally outmaneuver and ultimately dismantle the elusive network of AQI.

The challenges of our complex, fragmented world demand a new approach to organization— one that moves beyond traditional hierarchies to embrace agility and interconnectedness. General Stanley McChrystal's "Team of Teams" model offers a powerful framework for this, focusing on building trust and inspiring empowered action across interconnected teams. This model is built on two core principles: *shared consciousness and empowered execution.*[9]

1. Shared Consciousness: Fostering Collective Awareness
Shared consciousness is the "intelligence & understanding created by a collective view of the operating environment and a high level of internal connectivity."[9] It's more than just sharing information; it's about cultivating a common understanding of the Church's mission and the context in which it operates.

- *Be more loyal to the team you are in than the team you lead.* This principle challenges us to prioritize the unity of the entire church body over the loyalty to our specific ministry or team. When we align our efforts with the larger mission, we prevent the creation of silos and foster a more cohesive and effective community.

- *Brains, not just hands and wallets.* True empowerment means engaging people's intellectual gifts and creativity, not just their physical labor or financial contributions. By inviting people to contribute their ideas and participate in meaningful dialogue, we unlock the full potential of the congregation and build a more vibrant community.

2. Empowered Execution: Enabling Autonomy and Initiative
Empowered execution involves decentralizing decision-making to the teams and individuals closest to the work, allowing them to take ownership and initiative. This is not simply delegation, but a strategic release of authority rooted in trust and a shared purpose. The biblical example of Moses and Jethro in Exodus 18 illustrates this perfectly, showing how empowering leaders to judge minor cases was essential for sustainable and efficient leadership.

This uniquely empowers the Church and Christian mission organizations in today's complex, fragmented, and divided world. By fostering deep trust and understanding across diverse ministries and denominations, they can move beyond isolated efforts and respond with agility to rapidly changing societal needs. This approach allows for a more holistic and nuanced engagement, breaking down internal silos and external barriers, ultimately enabling a more effective and unified witness in reaching individuals and communities with compassion and relevance.

THE SELF-RELIANCE TRAP:
MOVING FROM INDEPENDENCE TO INTERDEPENDENCE

In a world that lionizes the "self-made" individual, it is little surprise that the Church and Christian organizations often fall prey to a culture of self-reliance. This is the mentality of the Lone Ranger: the gifted leader who believes they alone can carry the ministry's weight; the talented artist who works in isolation; the ministry that hoards its resources and knowledge, convinced its unique approach is the only way forward. While born from a place of passion and a desire for excellence, this culture of independence is a fundamental obstacle to building the kind of agile, resilient community needed to engage a complex world. True strength and sustainability are not found in the heroic individual but in a strategic shift from independence to interdependence.

This journey is not about abandoning your unique gifts, but about recognizing that they find their fullest expression when woven into the fabric of a collective. It's a move away from the isolated expert to the integrated team player, a principle embodied by three core tenets:

1. **The Body of Christ as a Shared Consciousness:** The Apostle Paul's powerful metaphor of the church as a single body with many members is not merely a poetic ideal; it is a blueprint for operational effectiveness. As Scripture states, "just as a body, though

one, has many parts, but all its many parts form one body, so it is with Christ" (1 Corinthians 12:12). This passage, along with Romans 12:4-5, explains that each part is essential and that we are mutually dependent on one another. Just as McChrystal's teams developed a "shared consciousness" by openly sharing information, the Body of Christ thrives when each part understands its role within the whole. The pastor knows their purpose is not to be the sole source of wisdom, but to be the connective tissue between diverse voices. The worship leader understands their gift is not for personal performance, but for the collective spiritual health of the community. This shift dismantles the silos of self-reliance, ensuring that every member—from the prayer warrior to the podcast editor—operates with a shared vision and a mutual reliance upon one another.

2. **The Strength of the Braided Rope:** A single strand of rope, no matter how strong, is easily frayed and broken. Its power is limited by its own circumference. But when multiple strands are braided together, they create a rope of exponential strength and resilience. The tension is distributed, the load is shared, and the collective is able to bear a weight that would have broken any individual part. This is the essence of interdependence in Christian mission, a principle echoed in Ecclesiastes 4:12— "Though one may be overpowered, two can defend themselves. A cord of three strands is not quickly broken." By intentionally interweaving gifts, resources, and even weaknesses, the Church becomes a more durable and adaptable force. It means the youth ministry doesn't operate in a vacuum but shares resources with the children's ministry. It means a seasoned elder actively mentors a new believer, creating a new strand of leadership. This collective strength is the antidote to the burnout that so often plagues the self-reliant leader.

3. **From Spectators to Participants:** The Priesthood of All Believers: The most profound skill for an interdependent community is the ability to empower others. The doctrine of the priesthood of all believers means the work of ministry is not reserved for a select few, but for every single member of the Body. In practice, this means moving away from a model where a few "professionals" do all the work while the majority are spectators. The interdependent leader's primary role is to equip people for ministry, as Ephesians 4:12 mandates, and then trust them to act. This decentralizes authority and action, creating a network of empowered, "on-the-ground" ministers who can respond with agility and creativity to the specific needs and challenges of their unique contexts. It is the ultimate rejection of self-reliance, building a community where everyone is a vital agent in the collective mission.

CREATING A TRANSFORMATIONAL ENVIRONMENT

Everything we do, we do in culture. There is no way for us to live or minister outside of it. Culture is to our lives what water is to a fish. As we've seen in the Blockbuster story, organizations that fail to understand the prevailing culture are destined to become irrelevant. Recognizing this, the Church has historically adopted different postures in its relationship with the surrounding culture.

Over the ages, the Church's response to culture has fallen mainly into one of three categories: imitate, isolate, or infiltrate. Some have chosen to imitate the dominant culture, adopting its customs, behaviors, and values to gain acceptance or fit in. While this may facilitate integration, it often leads to the dilution of the Church's unique identity and traditions. Others have chosen to isolate themselves from culture, maintaining a distance to preserve their identity and resist perceived threats. This approach, while providing a sense of security, can lead to marginalization, social exclusion, and a loss of influence on the world the Church is called to reach. A third response is to infiltrate the culture, actively participating in it with the intention of bringing about change. This model of engagement, where the Church influences values and norms while building bridges, is a potent path toward cultural transformation. As Romans 12:2 reminds us, our calling is not to conform to the world but to be transformed by the renewing of our minds so we may prove what God's good and perfect will is.

Today, the dominant force in our culture is consumerism. It's a social and economic system where people are driven to acquire goods and services beyond necessity, fueled by the belief that happiness is linked to consumption. The great danger for the Church is allowing this consumerist mindset to create a transactional culture within its own walls. A transactional loop is a system of "giving people what they want in exchange for what we want." It treats ministry like a business deal and faith like a product, where the Church provides programs, polished sermons, and engaging events, and the people, in turn, offer their attendance, loyalty, and resources.

This transactional culture is fundamentally at odds with the gospel's call to transformation. As leaders, we must break this transactional loop and instead cultivate a transformational loop where "changed people change people and society" is the driving force. A transactional environment is characterized by running a program of meetings, viewing people as spectators and consumers, and leaders who are served. The ultimate result is creating followers and loyal members. In contrast, a transformational environment focuses on facilitating a process of change, where people are seen as active participants and contributors. In this model, leaders serve—not to be served—but to cultivate more leaders and committed owners of the mission. This shift is crucial because, as 2 Corinthians 3:18 tells us, we are all being transformed into the image of the Lord, "from glory to glory, just as by the Spirit of the Lord." It is this profound process of personal and communal transformation that is the antidote to a consumer-driven culture.

Four Keys to accelerate a transformation culture in the midst of a transactional culture:

1. **Become the shoulders that others stand on.** This means adopting the posture of a "servant of all," rather than a leader who is served by others. It involves a shift in mindset where the leader's role is to elevate and empower others.

2. **Take the risk and pay the price for people to take the next step.** This requires leaders to see the potential in people, invest in developing their skills, and actively empower them into leadership. It is about creating an environment where growth is valued and leaders are willing to sacrifice for the development of others.

3. **Give away responsibility, not just tasks.** People own what they help design. This is a crucial distinction from the transactional approach of simply delegating tasks.

Transformational leadership involves empowering people with genuine ownership and responsibility, fostering a sense of co-creation and commitment.

4. **Attract consumers, but do not leave them that way.** The goal is not to repel those who are initially drawn in by a consumerist mindset, but to guide them on a journey from passive spectators to active participants. The transformation loop is a process that changes people, and it is the leader's role to facilitate that change.

Ultimately, these keys are designed to help leaders navigate a culture that often encourages imitation or isolation. Instead of conforming to the world's patterns or separating from it, transformational leaders are called to infiltrate culture with the intention of bringing about change. This requires actively participating while also seeking to influence its values and norms.

INCREMENTAL OBEDIENCE

Embracing incremental obedience means taking consistent, small steps in alignment with God's will, starting with personal transformation. This gradual faithfulness, rather than grand gestures, creates a ripple effect, fostering trust and ultimately inspiring positive change within the wider community.

Boshoff Grobler has lived most of his life in the world of macroeconomics—in investment banking, asset management, and the stability of "blue-chip" environments. For decades, he believed in the prevailing logic that "big is good." He shares that what once represented security and sustainability now feels increasingly irrelevant, and he's experiencing a "groundswell... a movement from the grassroots that's going to change the world." Making a shift from macro-influence to micro-stewardship requires more than strategy; it demands prophetic listening. Boshoff admits he once relied too heavily on his own expertise, hearing a word from God but then building a five-year budget around it, only to see it "fall flat." He has since learned to listen differently, committing to incremental obedience: "God works with me through progressive revelation. I've learned to take small steps in the direction of the light—even when I don't fully understand it." This posture of listening has also shaped his family, as he intentionally includes his adult children in decision-making, believing that the next generation must co-steward what God is doing.

"As he looks to the future, Boshoff believes we are entering an "apostolic age," where action must follow the past decades of prayer and prophetic resurgence. He states, "The Lord is calling people to make big moves—career shifts, ministry transitions, and bold, counter-cultural obedience." For some making a shift from macro to micro, the world might call it failure, but in the Kingdom, he smiles, "it's actually stepping up."

A LESSON FROM BLOCKBUSTER

The vast majority of those 9,000 Blockbuster stores are gone—relics of a bygone era. A single Blockbuster store remains in Bend, Oregon,[10] operating as a nostalgic curiosity, a living museum to a business model that simply couldn't adapt. It's a testament to what happens when an organization, no matter how successful, clings to old maps and familiar territory while the world around it undergoes a great unraveling. Netflix, on the other hand, became a global streaming powerhouse, a pioneer that understood the shifting dimensions of value, technology, and attention.

The story of Blockbuster isn't just about a failed business; it's a striking illustration of the challenges facing the Church in the *Shifting Dimensions of Organization*. Just as Blockbuster was proficient at hitting the ball it could see (physical rentals, late fees), the Church can become comfortable in its established practices, methods, and structures. But the world is rapidly redefining wealth, technology, automation, and what it means to be connected or self-sufficient. Like Blockbuster, the Church is being challenged to hold truth in tension—to discern what is core and unchangeable, and what organizational forms and methods need to be reinvented. It calls for the art of innovation, for the courage to let go of what no longer serves the mission, and the willingness to embrace collaborative and intergenerational leadership to build new paths forward.

If we, as Christian leaders, are to effectively "hit the ball we cannot yet see," we must learn from the echoes of past giants who failed to adapt. The lesson from Blockbuster isn't about ditching our mission, but about radically reshaping our methods, embracing new maps, and boldly pioneering into the future with Christ at the center, ensuring the enduring message of the gospel remains relevant in a rapidly unraveling world. Kristen Shuler reminds us that even as the mission grows more challenging and the cost becomes real, her outlook is far from defeatist—it carries the same profound hope echoed by East-West's founder John Maisel: "It's only going to get worse. But that just means it's time to go tell someone about Jesus."

EVERYTHING WE DO,
WE DO IN *CULTURE*.
THERE IS NO WAY
FOR US TO LIVE OR
MINISTER OUTSIDE
OF IT.
CULTURE IS TO OUR
LIVES WHAT WATER IS
TO A FISH.

CHAPTER 6 SUMMARY

This chapter uses the story of Blockbuster's demise to illustrate how organizations can fail when they cling to old models in a world that is undergoing a "great unraveling." It highlights key shifts like the widening chasms of wealth and technology, the automation reversal, and increasing self-sufficiency at both individual and national levels. These shifts create a fragmented, polarized landscape that traditional ministry models are ill-equipped to handle. The chapter calls for a new approach to organization rooted in collaboration, unity, and a "prophetic voice" that offers a middle-ground answer to extremist mentalities. It emphasizes empowering local leaders and embracing a posture of radical generosity and collaboration, moving away from empire-building toward community-building.

SKILL:
EMPOWER OTHERS THROUGH THE UTILIZATION AND GENERATION OF RESOURCES FOR GOOD

REFLECTIVE QUESTIONS

1. What old strategies (structures, strategies, assumptions) are no longer helpful for the terrain you're facing?

2. In what ways have you seen individual or national self-sufficiency affect your faith community?

3. Where are you modeling collaborative and intergenerational leadership, and where are you still stuck in hierarchy?

JOIN THE CONVERSATION
& WATCH THE INTERVIEWS HERE

PART 3

HOW WE CONNECT
(RELATIONAL)

THE MORE TAILORED
OUR WORLDS
BECOME TO 'YOU,'
THE MORE
ISOLATED 'YOU'
ULTIMATELY BECOME
FROM 'US.'

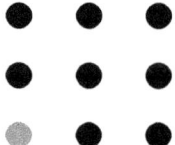

CHAPTER 7

SHIFTING DEGREES OF SEPARATION

In a world of frayed foundations and deteriorating institutions, the need for genuine connection has never been greater. This chapter, the first in our final two shifts, explores how technology has created a new *Paradox of Proximity*, where we are more connected than ever, yet more isolated and lonely. This is a profound connection rewiring, a fundamental change in how we relate to one another.

In the mid-20th century, a captivating question occupied the minds of social scientists: How interconnected is humanity, really? This question found its most famous exploration in the work of social psychologist Stanley Milgram, who, in 1963, conducted his groundbreaking "Small World Experiment"[1] at Harvard. His methodology was elegantly simple, yet profoundly insightful. He selected arbitrary "starting persons" in Nebraska and Boston and gave them a singular objective: get a document to a specific "target person" in Massachusetts by sending it only to a first-name acquaintance of the sender. Milgram's experiment sought to map the pathways along these acquaintance chains to determine the probability that any two people, even those seemingly far removed, could be connected through a series of intermediaries.

The results were astonishing and quickly entered the popular lexicon. Milgram's findings suggested that most people could successfully connect to a designated stranger with a chain of six or fewer links. This gave birth to the enduring phrase "Six Degrees of Separation,"[1] a concept that transcended academic circles to become the name of a play, a movie, and the inspiration for the popular "Six Degrees of Kevin Bacon" game. The enduring power of this simple idea lies in its intuitive appeal; it offers a comforting sense of proximity in a vast and complex world, suggesting that even strangers are not truly distant. This framework provided a relatable answer to a complex question about societal structure, setting the stage for how future generations would interpret connectivity, long before the advent of digital networks.

The dawn of the internet promised a new era of connection, and in 1997, a pioneering platform emerged that explicitly embodied Milgram's theory: SixDegrees.com.[2] Launched by Andrew Weinreich, it was widely recognized as the first social media network and was named directly after the "six degrees of separation" concept. SixDegrees. com introduced features that are now fundamental to online social interaction, such as personal profiles, friend lists that visually mapped connections, public message boards, and interest-based groups. At its peak, it boasted around one million registered users. Despite its short lifespan, SixDegrees.com laid the essential groundwork for the social media giants that would follow.[3]

The true quantitative re-evaluation of Milgram's theory arrived with the explosion of modern social media. Platforms like Facebook, with their massive user bases and computational power, could analyze connections on an unprecedented scale. In 2016, Facebook crunched its friend graph, encompassing 1.59 billion active users, and delivered a striking revelation: the average person was connected to every other person by an average of just 3.57 steps.[4] This represented a significant reduction from Milgram's six degrees and even a further compression from Facebook's own 2011 finding of 3.74 degrees, illustrating how increased network density can literally shrink the world. Professional networking platforms like LinkedIn also demonstrated this digital compression, albeit with different nuances. The average shortest path length for a central node on LinkedIn can be as low as 1.99, further underscoring the quantitative closeness enabled by digital platforms.[5]

This quantitative shrinking of the world, from Milgram's six degrees to Facebook's 3.57, represents a triumph of modern social networking and an acceleration in connectedness. However, it also highlights a critical qualitative shift. The reduction in "degrees of separation" primarily measures potential reach or network proximity, not the depth or quality of human relationships. While digital platforms boost connectivity, they often foster superficial connections, reducing the quality time spent in person and promoting a focus on virtual validation. Online friendships, for instance, are frequently perceived as less close and supportive, often being less developed and of shorter duration than face-to-face ties. The ease of forming numerous weak ties, where "friends" might even be strangers, can dilute emotional investment and create an "illusion of connection." This leads to a paradoxical outcome: increased access to connections does not necessarily translate into increased feelings of genuine connection.

This is the *Paradox of Proximity*—a world more connected than ever, yet more isolated. In an age where the world's population is theoretically more interconnected than at any point in human history, a profound and disturbing paradox has emerged: a global epidemic of loneliness and social disconnection.

SHIFTS:

HYPER-INDIVIDUALIZATION

This phenomenon of hyper-individualization is not merely a side effect but the ultimate culmination of the increasing separation and pervasive loneliness experienced in a hyper-connected world devoid of genuine depth. It is the bitter fruit of a tree planted in the soil of boundless choice and nurtured by algorithms that prioritize individual preference over communal experience. The *Paradox of Proximity* finds its starkest expression here: the more tailored our worlds become to "you," the more isolated "you" ultimately become from "us."

The Shift to You phenomenon, ushered in by platforms like YouTube, is at the heart of this paradox. Imagine the 1990s, a pre-digital era where the television screen served as a communal hearth. Families would gather to watch a handful of shared cultural touchstones like Seinfeld or the evening news. These weren't just shows; they were shared experiences, watercooler conversations in the making. The content was finite and consumed by a relatively passive audience.

Then came YouTube, and with it, a tipping point in the grand narrative of human connection and media consumption. It wasn't merely about putting videos online; it was about democratizing the means of production and distribution, an alchemy that transmuted passive viewers into active creators, and then back again, in an endless, self-sustaining loop. The amount of content uploaded to YouTube in a single year today dwarfs the output of the entire television industry in the 1990s. This explosion of content was not accidental; it tapped into a deep human desire to be seen, to be heard, and to connect—but on one's own terms.

This is the *Shift to You* phenomenon: the empowerment of the individual as both the arbiter and the architect of their media landscape. The communal hearth of the 90s has been shattered into a million individualized shards, each reflecting a unique, meticulously curated digital universe. We no longer gather; we delve. Each person is immersed in a bespoke stream of content, tailored by sophisticated algorithms that anticipate our desires and push us deeper into our niche interests, reinforcing our existing biases and perfecting the echo chamber.

This amplification of individualism has created a "post-community society," where shared cultural experiences are eroding and individuals are increasingly isolated within their own perfectly tailored digital bubbles. The very tool designed to bring us closer, to offer unprecedented choice and personalization, might just be intensifying a new form of solitude, a silent testament to the unintended consequences of boundless choice.
Social media's "highlight reel" culture cultivates an illusion of intimacy while exacting a heavy psychological toll. This constant exposure to idealized realities can lead to feelings of inadequacy, comparison, and dissatisfaction, particularly among younger generations like Gen Z, where 41% report facing mental health challenges linked to this constant comparison. The "Fear of Missing Out" (FOMO) has become a pervasive anxiety, driving compulsive checking of social media sites and negatively impacting mental health. The pursuit of external validation, manifested in the "dopamine hit" from likes and comments, creates an addictive feedback loop that prioritizes digital approval over genuine connection. This digital addiction can reduce the quality of time individuals spend with those who are physically present.

Further complicating the landscape of connection is the societal narrative surrounding solitude. University of Michigan research highlights that the media often portrays being alone as inherently negative or dangerous, with stories ten times more likely to describe it as harmful than beneficial.[6] This well-intentioned public discourse, aimed at combating loneliness, can backfire, as individuals who internalize these negative beliefs tend to feel lonelier after spending time alone. This suggests that the problem is not just the lack of connection, but the type of connection being fostered and the mindset it cultivates.[6]

Hikikomori, a term coined in Japan, describes a severe form of social withdrawal where individuals isolate themselves, often remaining confined to their rooms for extended periods, even years, and severing most, if not all, social connections. While originating in Japan, this phenomenon is now recognized as a growing global concern.[7]

The scale of Hikikomori in Japan is particularly striking. A March 2023 survey by the Japanese Cabinet Office estimated that approximately 1.46 million people, or 2% of the Japanese population aged 15 to 64, could be living as Hikikomori.[8] This extreme manifestation of isolation serves as a powerful warning for increasingly isolated societies worldwide, reflecting the fragile nature of human connection in modern life. It highlights the paradox of hyper-connectivity coexisting with profound isolation.

YOUNG PEOPLE ARE LEAVING TRADITIONAL CHURCH STRUCTURES AT HIGHER RATES BECAUSE THEY DON'T SEE *THEMSELVES* OR THE KIND OF *COLLABORATIVE LEADERSHIP* THEY VALUE *REFLECTED* THERE.

IMPACT ON JESUS-FOLLOWING:

This hyper-individualization has significant and troubling impacts on the Church and the proclamation of the gospel. It creates a relevance deficit that can lead to spiritual skepticism, and even atheism, among those observing from the outside. This is because the world observes division, distrust, and separation within the very body that claims to represent Jesus. When the Church fails to overcome its own disconnections and, instead, conforms to a society characterized by fragmentation and hyper-individualism, it loses its distinctiveness and its compelling power.

LOVING JESUS BUT DISTRUSTING THE CHURCH

Dan Blythe, Global Youth Director for Alpha, notes a critical shift: a generation that "loves Jesus" often "doesn't trust the Church." This distrust stems from a desire for authentic, vulnerable leadership that stands in stark contrast to the perceived need for "perfect performance" often amplified by digital culture. For young people, the Church is a place where they feel they can't ask questions or wrestle with doubt. They are looking for "vulnerable leadership and honest answers—even if the answer is, 'I don't know, but let's find out together.'" In a world oversaturated with filters and branding, Gen Z is starving for what's real. They see Jesus as authentic but are waiting to see if the Church will be too.

Young people are leaving traditional church structures at higher rates because they don't see themselves or the kind of collaborative leadership they value reflected there. As Jenn Brown, a leader in one of the most innovative Bible engagement strategies for the next generation, points out, research shows that for the first time, 18-24-year-old women are leaving the Church at higher rates than men.[9] They are "walking away from structures where they can't see themselves." Young women are finding empowerment and belonging in society, but often not in the Church. This is not just a crisis, but a signal that collaborative leadership is a necessary response to the longings of a generation.

DIVISION IN THE CHURCH CAUSES ATHEISM IN THE WORLD

Jesus prayed for the unity of believers in John 17:21 NIV: "That they may all be one... so that the world may believe that you have sent me." This profound statement reveals that the unity of believers is not merely an internal preference, but a powerful, external witness to the world of Christ's divine mission. The inverse is also tragically true: when the world observes division, distrust, and separation within the very body that claims to represent Him, the result is often deepening cynicism and a dismissal of the Christian message as irrelevant or hypocritical.

Terry Parkman poignantly reminds us that global proximity does not equal unity. "The Body of Christ is triggered when we are unified around truth. Not just unified for unity's sake." He believes we're watching a deconstruction—not just of celebrity Christianity, but of ideological silos. And yet, in that unraveling, new "digital campfires" are forming—places where ideas, theology, and tribes gather online. "The challenge," he says, "is to make those digital campfires inclusive, humble, open to dialogue—not echo chambers. Otherwise, you're just weaponizing your perspective."

SUPERFICIAL ENGAGEMENT VS. DEEP DISCIPLESHIP

The "illusion of connection" fostered by digital platforms can lead to a similar superficiality in church life. People may be "connected" online or attend a service in a "row," but they lack the deep, meaningful relationships and commitment necessary for true discipleship and communal growth. This is the difference between treating church like a "restaurant" where you show up and get fed, and seeing it as a "home" where you take ownership and have work to do. The younger generation is looking to build, not just to belong. If we don't give them bricks, they will build with whatever culture offers them. The gospel doesn't ignore the pain of the world; it speaks to it and bleeds for it. This generation wants to act on justice, and if the Church doesn't move fast enough, they'll take action themselves.

THE UNSEEN THREAT OF FRAGMENTATION

The Shift to You phenomenon, marked by an amplification of individualism, creates a "post-community society." If the Church mirrors this isolation rather than countering it with radical, self-sacrificing unity, it becomes just another echo of the world's brokenness, rather than a transformative force. This fragmentation is also a struggle of the self. As China marketing strategist Kevin Lee observes, young people are juggling multiple accounts and personas across platforms, leaving little room for a unified sense of self. They may feel authentic in each space, yet remain unsure of who they truly are—resulting in a quiet, persistent existential ache. This generation isn't faking an identity; they simply haven't learned how to weave together the many versions of themselves into a coherent whole.

This fragmentation extends to relationships. With the rise of AI companions, which are built to be agreeable and conflict-free, millions are losing the very human friction of "conflict and compromise" that shapes us. The Church has a crucial role to play in fostering real relationships that offer the depth, accountability, and transformative friction that digital connections often lack.

SKILLS:

In a world defined by shifting degrees of separation and a pervasive paradox of proximity, the Church is called to master a set of skills that rebuild authentic connection. We've seen how the digital age, while collapsing distances, has simultaneously fueled hyper-individualism and a deep-seated loneliness. To counteract this, we must intentionally cultivate skills that move people from passive existence to active participation, from transactional relationships to transformational community.

COLLABORATION AND INTERDEPENDENCE

The myth that we can go at it alone must be replaced by a profound belief that we're *better together*. The metaphor of draft horses powerfully illustrates this: one horse can pull about 8,000 pounds, but two working together can pull not 16,000, but up to 24,000 pounds. When trained to lean on each other's strengths, they can pull up to 32,000 pounds. Two horses can do the work of four when truly collaborating. This synergy is what Jesus had in mind when he prayed for unity in John 17.

Collaboration is not a mere buzzword but a spiritual imperative, and it's the only way to effectively mobilize and reach the next generation. As Jenn points out, "real collaboration takes more. It takes translated models, contextual application, and long-haul commitment." It is a call to "contending for kingdom outcomes together."

A generation is rising that is desperately seeking something substantial to give their lives for—a cause, a force, a truth worth laying down differences and coming together in profound unity. If the Church, instead of offering this beacon of cohesive purpose, presents a fractured image rife with internal squabbles and theological disputes, it will inevitably fail to capture the hearts and minds of those searching for genuine meaning. The Church must reclaim its calling to be a body of unified, collaborative believers. This is a spiritual imperative, not just a strategic maneuver.

This requires a new kind of leadership—one that is interdependent, interconnected, and shared. The "leader of the future," Jenn says, "is the one who doesn't need to be seen." This challenges traditional, individualistic leadership models and aligns with the shift toward interdependence. This kind of leadership is often intuitive for women, and embracing it is not just a trend but a necessary response to a generation that is walking away from structures where they can't see themselves.

ROWS CAN'T ASK QUESTIONS.
ROWS CAN'T WRESTLE WITH DOUBT.
ROWS CAN'T BUILD TRUST.
CIRCLES CAN.

DAN BLYTHE

CIRCLES, NOT ROWS

The future of faith will be defined not by how well we fill stadiums, but by how well we gather in circles. We have spent decades perfecting the art of "rows" – organizing large services, delivering polished sermons, and creating seamless events where people sit and listen. While these have their place, rows are a structure built for passive consumption, not for active participation. As Dan Blythe points out, "Rows can't ask questions. Rows can't wrestle with doubt. Rows can't build trust. Circles can." The younger generation, in particular, is not content to be a silent audience; they have "ten questions for every point in a sermon" and a profound desire to "sit and discuss." Circles—whether small groups, dinner tables, or spontaneous hangouts—are the spaces where authentic community and personal discipleship happen.

These circles must be intergenerational, led by authentic presence rather than charisma, and be a safe space to ask questions without judgment. Dan Blythe challenges the myth that youth ministry is about being cool or trendy; "Gen Z doesn't need a cool youth pastor," he says, "They need someone who shows up, remembers their name, listens, and loves them." This shift isn't just about small groups; it affects how we think about the Church as a whole. Community must be more than an event; it must be a culture—a network of circles where people are seen, heard, known, and discipled.

This shift from rows to circles requires a fundamental change in our understanding of leadership and community. It demands vulnerable leadership and honest answers. This generation is starving for what's real and is not looking for a perfect performance. They love Jesus, whom they see as authentic, but many "don't trust the Church" and are waiting to see if the Church will be authentic, too. Leaders must be willing to admit when they "don't know, but let's find out together." This is what builds trust, and trust is the fertile ground in which true belonging can grow.

It is crucial to understand that this call for 'circles' is not a declaration against 'rows.' The proclamation of God's Word in larger gatherings, the unified experience of corporate worship, and the powerful witness of a congregation gathered together are irreplaceable and vital aspects of the Church's life. Rows have immense value. The argument is not for the abolition of rows, but for the intentional cultivation of circles alongside them. In an age marked by profound isolation, rows alone are insufficient to combat the loneliness epidemic. While rows can inform and inspire, it is in circles where deep connection is forged, where trust is built, and where true belonging is discovered. We must see them not as competing models, but as essential, complementary environments for a healthy, thriving church.

A THEOLOGY FOR COLLABORATION

To truly address the shift toward hyper-individualism, the Church must develop a theology for collaboration, moving beyond simply quoting John 17 to actually living it out. This means creating a "micro-consortia" of like-minded organizations and individuals to tackle specific problems and recognize that a new kind of collaborative leadership is required. Jenn sees bright spots not in large-scale movements but in these small groups of two, three, or four organizations collaborating around one problem, one question, or one shared goal. These models are leaner, more focused, and often more fruitful. She calls for "architects of connection"—dedicated people who actively match people and projects, forming bridges between aligned missions and emerging needs.

The power of this collaboration is rooted in a shared "bull's-eye"—Jesus at the center—which allows for unity and collaboration despite outer boundary disagreements. When we keep Jesus at the center, we can focus on core essentials and apply relational skills to navigate differences amidst strongly held convictions. This approach, as Michael A. Ortiz describes, helps the Church recover its original role as a melting pot of cultures—a level playing field where every voice matters, echoing the vision of Acts 2, where people heard the gospel in their own language.

THE IRREDUCIBLE MODEL OF TRANSFORMATIONAL COMMUNITY

Building authentic community in a fragmented world is a counter-cultural process that requires moving beyond transactional relationships, which are rooted in exchange and short-term outcomes, to transformational relationships, which are based on mutual growth and shared purpose. This migration is not easy; it runs against a societal tide that prizes efficiency over depth. However, by focusing on a shared vision, fostering vulnerable communication, and committing to long-term engagement, we can transcend superficial interactions and cultivate a community that is genuinely transformative.

This journey from transactional to transformational can be understood through an "irreducible model" with four key stages, each building upon the last to create a foundation for accelerated local fruitfulness and momentum.

1. Conversion to Unity (The Invite)
The first step in building a transformational community is the invitation to unity. This is the moment when an individual is called out of their isolation and into a shared faith, anchored by the gospel. This stage is characterized by a compelling vision that is bigger than any single person, emphasizing the power of "we" over "me." It's an inclusive invitation to join a collective journey, fostering a sense of spiritual formation and shared identity in Christ.

2. Meaningful Convening & Connection (Come Together)
Once the invitation is accepted, the community must create spaces for genuine connection. This stage is about moving from the theoretical idea of "together" to the practical experience of it. It requires meaningful convening through activities like small groups, fellowship events, and intergenerational activities that bring people together face-to-face. Mentorship programs and shared experiences, such as missions or service projects, are crucial in this stage for deepening bonds and fostering emotional intimacy.

3. Discovering the Power of Collaboration (Work Together)
True belonging is discovered not just in being with others, but in working with them toward a common goal. This stage is about moving from passive participation to active collaboration, where individuals discover their unique roles and contributions within

the community. This can be expressed through ministry involvement, team projects, and shared leadership, all while appreciating the diversity of gifts and perspectives within the body. The focus shifts from individual effort to collective impact, building a sense of shared ownership and purpose that strengthens the community's bonds. As Jenn states, "The Church is still quoting John 17 without knowing how to live it," and "We've been inoculated by images of collaboration. But God's vision for it is way deeper than we've dared to imagine."

4. Accelerated Local Fruitfulness & Building Momentum (See Local Increase)
The culmination of these stages is a vibrant, healthy community that begins to see tangible results of its efforts. This fruitfulness can manifest in spiritual growth, increased engagement, and a powerful impact on the surrounding community. It also leads to a renewed passion and a natural momentum that attracts others, perpetuating a cycle of growth and transformation. This is the ultimate goal: a community that is not just surviving but thriving, a beacon of hope in a world of profound disconnection.

CULTIVATING A HEALTHY COMMUNITY: RHYTHM, ROUTINE, AND RITUALS

A community is only as strong as its health. In a world of increasing busyness and distraction, fostering a healthy community requires intentionality around three core practices: rhythm, routine, and ritual.

1. Rhythm (Finding Our Pace)
The modern world is obsessed with speed and productivity. However, a healthy community operates on a different clock. It recognizes that life has seasons and that there is a time for activity and a time for rest. A thriving fellowship intentionally adjusts its pace, finding its unique rhythm of connection and meeting. This regularity of engagement deepens relationships and creates a sense of safety, preventing burnout and fostering a sustainable, long-term approach to life together.

2. Routine (Forming Good Habits)
Routine provides the structure that supports a healthy community. These are the consistent practices that nurture spiritual growth and connection, such as regular worship, small group meetings, and discipleship. Routines create a predictable environment where people can feel safe and supported, even amidst the chaos of a changing world. They are the glue that holds the community together, ensuring that the fundamental habits of faith are consistently practiced and reinforced.

3. Rituals (Building Monuments)
Rituals are the meaningful practices that connect the community to its core values and faith story. They are moments of shared memory and spiritual significance that transcend the everyday. Communion, baptism, seasonal celebrations, prayer, and even simple acts like having coffee together are all rituals that serve as "monuments" of the community's journey, grounding them in a shared history and a common identity. In a world where meaning is often fleeting, rituals provide an anchor, reminding the community of who they are and whose they are.

RAISING HIGH-CAPACITY LEADERS

Transformational communities do not happen by accident; they are built and led by transformational leaders. In the face of a fragmented world, raising high-capacity leaders is essential for the future of faith. This requires a new approach to leadership development, one that focuses on four key areas: **Value, Vision, Vehicle, and Involvement.**

- **Value (Application):** High-capacity leaders deeply understand and embody our core values. This point, however, deals more with their value; leaders are asking, "Is it worth my time?" Leaders who feel valued and believe their time is worthwhile are more likely to embody and promote core values within their teams authentically. What gets celebrated gets replicated, but who gets celebrated gets multiplied.

- **Vision (Alignment):** Leaders must be aligned with the overall vision and strategic direction of the community. They are asking, "Am I making a difference?" We need to develop our leaders' strategic thinking skills, helping them understand how their work links and contributes to the bigger picture.

- **Vehicles (Arranged Systems):** Leaders need the right systems, structures, and resources to succeed. They are asking, "How does it work?" This includes organizational design, resource allocation, and the effective use of technology. High-capacity leaders are frustrated when things are ineffective.

- **Involvement (Association):** High-capacity leaders must be actively engaged and connected with the people they serve. They are asking, "Who am I doing this with?" Relationship building, effective communication, and delegation are essential skills. The depth of relational connection is directly related to the longevity of engagement.

The future of faith will not be won through a new program or a single leader, but through a movement of deeply connected, collaborative, and healthy communities led by high-capacity leaders who are prepared to navigate the complexities of our age. By mastering the skills to build transformational community and developing leaders who embody its values, we can reclaim the deep truth that we are "better together" and advance the gospel in a world that is desperate for genuine connection.

A LESSON FROM PICKLEBALL

The world we inhabit today is a paradox: a world of collapsed distances and profound emotional isolation. The degrees of separation that once felt so vast have been collapsed by technology to an average of just 3.57 steps, yet the very tools designed to connect us have intensified our hyper-individualism and emotional distance. The Church stands at a critical juncture, faced with a significant spiritual and social need for authentic connection and unity. The old game, played in a world of "rows" and professional perfection, is no longer reaching a generation that is starving for what is real.

To find our way forward, we must look not to the established giants of the past, but to the game-changing disruptions of the present. For decades, tennis has been a global titan of sport, a game of individual prowess, massive prize money, and a highly professionalized industry. It is a spectacle of elite athleticism, played by a few for the admiration of millions. Yet, its very grandeur and high barriers to entry have created a perceived exclusivity that excludes and prohibits many from playing. The high physical demands, expensive equipment, and time-intensive training have made tennis a game for the few, not the many. It is, in many ways, a perfect metaphor for the "rows" we have perfected in our churches—a space for polished performance where people sit, watch, and admire, but rarely participate in the messy, joyful work of community.

But a revolution is underway on side courts and in converted gymnasiums around the world. It is a revolution led by two simple, accessible sports: pickleball and padel. In just a few short years, pickleball has become America's fastest-growing sport, with participation increasing by an astonishing 311% between 2021 and 2024.[10] Similarly, padel has seen exponential growth, with the number of courts worldwide surging from 21,000 to over 70,000 since 2018.[10] These sports are not succeeding because of multi-million dollar contracts or stadium-sized spectacles; they are succeeding because they have restored the core reason humans play games: togetherness.

Pickleball and padel are inherently social, communal, and fun. They have low barriers to entry, are easy to learn, and require minimal equipment, making them accessible to people of all ages and fitness levels. They prioritize camaraderie and social interaction over hyper-competitive individualism. This disruption mirrors the market-changing shifts of companies like Uber and Airbnb, which succeeded by restoring a lost value—the accessible, communal, and user-friendly nature of their services. In a world grappling with a profound sense of loneliness and hyper-individualism, these sports provide a tangible antidote, fulfilling the deep human need for belonging that algorithms and highlight reels cannot.

THE *GOSPEL* ADVANCES AT THE RATE OF *RELATIONSHIP*.

This is the Church's game-changing play: to be less like professional tennis and more like pickleball and padel. It's a call to restore the fun, authentic, and collaborative nature of being the Church that would cause millions to come and play again, not just sit on the couch and watch. It means moving from the passive consumption of "rows" to the active participation of "circles," where people are seen, known, and discipled in a genuine, messy community.

As Dan Blythe reminds us, young people don't need a cool youth pastor; "they need someone who shows up, remembers their name, listens, and loves them." This is the essence of a pickleball-style church—a place of authentic presence, not polished performance.

The task before us is too great to be carried alone. We must embrace a radical, collaborative unity, rooted in a shared purpose with Jesus at the center. This is what Jenn calls a "theology for collaboration"—one that moves beyond just quoting John 17 to actually living it out. This is the way we overcome the "separation paradox," where we are separated by less but feel more separated than ever. Just as draft horses achieve more together than they could ever accomplish alone, so the Church, unified in its love for Jesus and one another, can fulfill a mission that is far too big for any single individual or institution.

In a world yearning for authentic connection, our unity becomes the most powerful witness to the love of Christ. The gospel advances at the rate of relationship. This is not just about staying relevant; it is about following the way of Jesus, who himself demonstrated that our love for one another is the undeniable sign of His presence. It is time to step off the sidelines, put down our curated personas, and begin to play the new game—a game of authentic community, radical collaboration, and genuine joy that anyone, no matter their skill level, can get in on.

CHAPTER 7 SUMMARY

This chapter explores the paradox of a world that is more interconnected than ever, yet also more isolated. It traces the concept of "Six Degrees of Separation" from a social experiment to a digital reality where the average connection is now just 3.57 steps, yet loneliness is a global epidemic. The cause of this paradox of proximity is identified as "hyper-individualization" and the Shift to You phenomenon, which has replaced shared communal experiences with curated, digital-first realities. The chapter challenges the Church to move from passive "rows" to active "circles," fostering intergenerational community, collaborative leadership, and a "theology of collaboration." It uses the analogy of pickleball and padel to call for a church that is accessible, social, and centered on genuine, messy community rather than polished performance.

SKILL:
ELEVATE VOICES WITH A SHARED MESSAGE
BIGGER THAN THEMSELVES

REFLECTIVE QUESTIONS

1. How has hyperconnectivity changed your understanding of community—and what have you lost in the process?

2. What does collaboration look like in your current sphere of influence—and what's holding it back?

3. What would it look like to prioritize unity over uniformity in your context?

JOIN THE CONVERSATION
& WATCH THE INTERVIEWS HERE

THE *CHURCH*
IS THE CHURCH
ONLY WHEN IT EXISTS
FOR OTHERS.

DIETRICH BONHOEFFER

CHAPTER 8

SHIFTING DISCOVERY OF BELONGING

In a world that often feels fractured and isolating, the deep-rooted human need for belonging is more pressing than ever. The Church, when it lives out its true purpose, is uniquely positioned to answer this fundamental question of belonging, not by creating an exclusive club, but by becoming a beacon of radical, outward-focused love. This chapter provides the blueprint for a true, authentic reconnection, moving beyond passive observation to active, committed participation.

From the bustling, sun-drenched agoras of ancient Greece to the smoke-filled, spirited coffeehouses of 17th-century London, humanity has always sought refuge in a space beyond the confines of home and the demands of work. Sociologist Ray Oldenburg[1] coined this phenomenon the "third place," a neutral ground where social status dissolved and conversation was the main currency.[1] These were the beating hearts of the community— where the baker could debate with the philosopher and the merchant could mingle with the scholar. They were vibrant, accessible hubs that fostered a profound sense of belonging and were vital to the health of civic life itself.

For centuries, the Church was the quintessential third place by default in many cultures. It was the central anchor of community life, a space where people gathered not just for worship but also for social leveling, shared rituals, and collective support. It provided a powerful sense of identity and a ready-made social infrastructure that was as essential as the village square or the local tavern.

But the ground has shifted beneath our feet. The forces of industrialization and suburbanization systematically dismantled these traditional communal anchors, replacing them with a landscape of isolated homes and car-dependent sprawl. This physical separation was the first act in a great unraveling. The digital age, promising to restore connection, has ironically accelerated this fragmentation. As we've explored, it has given rise to the "alone together" phenomenon, where we share physical space but retreat into our digital cocoons.

In this new world, the Church, too, has been profoundly affected. In a frantic bid for relevance, many congregations have inadvertently abandoned their role as a third place. They have become less like the vibrant agoras of old and more like polished entertainment venues or information services. With slick productions and professional sermons, they've leaned heavily into performance—building environments designed for observation rather than participation. In doing so, they have traded the costly, tangible act of fostering belonging for the safer, more manageable business of providing content. This leaves a generation, starved for genuine connection, wondering: if the church is no longer a place for community, where can I possibly belong in such a disconnected world?

But the truth is, the Church is uniquely positioned to meet this longing—not through polished performance, but through genuine, Spirit-led presence. This is a call to cultivate environments where individuals can personally experience God, and where transformation flows from genuine community and divine encounter. This chapter will explore this critical shift, examining how the church can reclaim its ancient calling to be a true third place—a hub of authentic, life-giving belonging for a world in desperate need.

SHIFTS:

The human heart is hardwired for belonging. We are not designed for isolation, yet in a world of unprecedented digital hyper-connectivity, a profound and pervasive loneliness has become a silent epidemic. The World Health Organization (WHO) has issued a significant warning regarding a global "loneliness epidemic," identifying it as a pressing public health threat. This crisis is evidenced by alarming statistics, with over 871,000 deaths annually attributed to the direct and indirect effects of loneliness,[2] a figure comparable to global death tolls from major diseases such as heart conditions and diabetes. Loneliness is not merely the state of being alone but rather the painful sensation of emotional or social disconnection, representing a significant disparity between the relationships individuals possess and those they desire. Extensive research links loneliness to a wide array of adverse health outcomes, including impaired cognitive function, depression, anxiety, increased suicide risk, and premature mortality.[3] Conversely, strong social connections function as a "biological buffer," contributing to reduced inflammation, regulated stress hormones, improved mental well-being, and potentially extended life expectancy.[4] This global health crisis underscores a deep-seated human yearning for authentic community and belonging.

The underlying causes of this widespread disconnection extend beyond mere screen time. The loneliness crisis is deeply embedded in a complex web of socioeconomic and cultural factors. These include poor health and disabilities, economic hardships, the diminishing of traditional community spaces, a prevailing culture of hyper-independence, and a lack of accessible education and shared social infrastructure. Furthermore, loneliness is prevalent across all generations, with younger individuals (Generation Z) frequently reporting the highest average loneliness scores.[5] This trend is potentially linked to high social media engagement and reduced in-person communication.[5] The prevalence of deep disconnection amidst pervasive digital access highlights a critical observation: the issue is not simply a lack of physical presence, but a perceived absence of quality and emotional connection in relationships. Digital interactions, while offering a quantity of contact, frequently fall short in providing the quality of interaction vital for authentic belonging. The church, by its inherent nature, offers a space for authentic, in-person, and emotionally significant relationships that digital platforms struggle to replicate.

This spiritual deficit is compounded by the Shift to You phenomenon, which allows for an individualized and curated digital existence and has intensified hyper-individualism. It has shattered the communal hearth into "a million individualized shards" and created a "post-community society." The result is a generation drowning in "curated loneliness" and an innate, existential ache. People are not just looking for a place to be seen; they are asking a fundamental question about their existence: "Where do I truly belong?"

The Church, in many contexts, has struggled to keep up with these shifts. We have perfected the art of "rows" —large gatherings, polished sermons, and organized events. However, rows are a structure built for passive consumption and struggle to create space for the kind of messy, authentic community that fosters the deep relationships a lonely world is desperately seeking. They are a model for a world that has largely passed. The post-pandemic landscape, where only 67% of U.S. churchgoers returned to in-person attendance, has not caused a problem as much as it has exposed one: many pre-pandemic churchgoers have become consumers of church rather than active participants.[6] Therefore, the call of the hour is to commit to community—to move from passively spectating church to actively embodying what it means to *be* the Church.

IMPACT ON JESUS-FOLLOWING:

A CHURCH DISCONNECTED FROM ITS PURPOSE

The challenges of a lonely and consumer-driven world have greatly impacted the Church's ability to fulfill its mission, leading it to become increasingly disconnected from its original purpose.

A crucial part of creating authentic belonging is moving beyond a mindset of scarcity and control, which often leads to a defensive, inward-focused church. We must actively reject what Boshoff Grobler calls "empire thinking." This model, deeply embedded in our politics and economics, is rooted in scarcity, control, and self-preservation. Instead, the Church is called to model "Kingdom thinking," which is rooted in sufficiency, community, and belonging. This isn't about endless abundance but a profound belief that "there is enough for everyone" when we operate with generosity and trust. For Boshoff, the future of the Church must be about community-building, not institutional dominance. This radical generosity and restorative belonging is a direct antidote to the loneliness and fragmentation of our age.

LOSING THE "WHY": A PEOPLE NOT AN INSTITUTION

For many, the perception of the Church is that of a "poor, feeble, boring, petty, bourgeois institution." This was the view of Dietrich Bonhoeffer's brother when Bonhoeffer, at the age of 14, decided to become a pastor. Bonhoeffer's response was a defiant and prophetic one: "If what you say is true, I shall reform it!" His life became a testament to this conviction. Bonhoeffer believed the Church is only the Church when it "exists for others." It is not meant to dominate, but to help and serve. At its core, the Church is "people together as His body for others." This definition immediately shifts our focus from buildings, organizations, or brands to the people themselves. The Church is not a building it meets in, but the people who meet.

When the Church becomes about what it isn't—an institution, a business, or a social club—it loses its way and ceases to function as it was initially intended. The "church hurt" that so many have experienced is often a result of people forgetting that the church exists for people, not the other way around. The Sabbath, Jesus taught, was never meant to be a requirement for people to fulfill, but a rhythm designed for their flourishing (Mark 2:27). In the same way, the church exists for people, and people are not meant to serve the institution of the church. Peter reinforces this understanding by describing the church as a "spiritual house" built from "living stones." We, as believers, are these "living stones," being built up with Christ as the chief "brick" or cornerstone. The people make the church; people are the Church! Each of us forms a vital part of this spiritual structure, which is far more than a physical building. This is the essence of belonging—being a part of something larger than yourself, where your unique contribution is essential to the whole.

THE CHURCH IS NOT A *BUILDING* IT MEETS IN, BUT THE *PEOPLE* WHO MEET.

It is crucial to clarify that the emphasis on cultivating genuine community and individual belonging is not a critique of large churches or a call for smaller congregations. On the contrary, the vision is for churches of all sizes to embody these principles. The more people a church can reach, and the larger it can grow, while simultaneously retaining and fostering an authentic sense of community and profound belonging for each individual, the more effectively it will fulfill its divine purpose in a fractured world. The goal is not to limit scale, but to ensure that scale serves the depth of connection, rather than detracting from it.

THE DEHUMANIZED CROWD

In Mark chapter 8, the gospel presents a striking image where a blind man, after Jesus's initial touch, reports seeing "people as if they were trees walking." This blurry vision serves as a powerful metaphor for a common challenge faced by contemporary churches. The tendency to view congregants as a collective "crowd" rather than distinct persons can be understood as a theological blind spot. Jesus Himself did not prioritize crowd numbers in the way modern institutions often do, suggesting that the Church's preoccupation with attendance metrics and large-scale programs may represent a fundamental misapplication of divine priorities.

This blurred vision signifies a fundamental failure to recognize people's distinct personhood, their rich inner lives, personal struggles, or inherent potential. When churches focus on "crowds" rather than "individuals," they risk inadvertently dehumanizing their congregants, reducing them to mere statistics or passive recipients of ministry. Instead, they should be recognized as active, unique participants in the body of Christ—each an image bearer of God, a living stone carrying a unique and essential part in the spiritual house being built.

The blind man's initial partial vision, where he saw "people as if they were trees walking," directly parallels the disciples' partial spiritual vision. They were physically present with Jesus, witnessing His miracles and hearing his teachings, yet their comprehension of His messianic identity and the Kingdom of God remained blurry and incomplete. This deliberate imperfection of the first touch, necessitating a second, is not a limitation of Jesus's power but a significant pedagogical act. It teaches that spiritual growth and the comprehension of profound truths are often incremental journeys, requiring multiple "touches" or encounters with divine revelation. This implies that churches should embrace a process-oriented view of discipleship, acknowledging that individuals will have partial understanding and need ongoing guidance, rather than expecting immediate, perfect comprehension or "one-and-done" conversions.

A CHURCH THAT PRIORITIZES ITS OWN COMFORT OR SURVIVAL OVER A COSTLY ENGAGEMENT WITH THE WORLD'S SUFFERING INEVITABLY FAILS TO CREATE *TRUE BELONGING*.

Don't settle for seeing "people like trees." Instead, ask God to open your eyes to see each person through the lens of His design—uniquely created, deeply known, and purposed to play a vital role in the Church.

A RETREAT FROM MISSION

The essence of the Church's purpose is to exist "for others." This is the "so what?" of our faith. Yet a consumer-driven mindset has caused many churches to retreat from this outward mission, transforming the church into a place of comfort and passive observation. A lot of pre-pandemic churchgoers have moved away from being the church and have become consumers of church.

This inward focus and "religious consumerism" stemmed from a critique of "cheap grace" and the "inwardly oriented" church that Bonhoeffer saw in his time. "Cheap grace," he argued, is "the grace we bestow on ourselves,"—"forgiveness without requiring repentance, baptism without church discipline, Communion without confession, absolution without personal confession." This form of grace, detached from genuine discipleship, leads to a superficial faith and a focus on self-preservation.

This self-preservation, fostered by a diluted understanding of grace, resulted in the Church losing its capacity to bring "reconciliation and redemption" to humanity and its prophetic voice against injustice. A church that prioritizes its own comfort or survival over a costly engagement with the world's suffering inevitably fails to create true belonging. This historical lesson implies that the contemporary "loneliness epidemic" might, in part, be a consequence of the Church's historical retreat from its foundational missional calling. In a world desperate for connection, the Church's retreat from mission and its shift to a consumer-centric model have made it increasingly irrelevant to those seeking a genuine community and a purpose bigger than themselves.

SKILLS:

CULTIVATING CLEAR VISION AND AUTHENTIC COMMUNITY

To combat the pervasive loneliness and consumerism of our age, the Church must develop specific skills that move people from passive spectatorship to active participation, from transactional relationships to transformational community.

EMBODYING A COMMITTED COMMUNITY

The essence of a committed community can be found in the very definition of the Church. The Greek word for church is *Ecclesia*, a combination of two words: *Ek*, meaning "out of," and *Kaleo*, meaning "called" or "for a purpose." Therefore, the Church is not merely a gathering of people but an "assembly called for a purpose." This is a fundamental and often forgotten truth. The Church is meant to be a missional, active body, not a passive audience.

Being part of a true church community requires more than involvement; it requires commitment. The well-known analogy of a chicken and a pig starting a breakfast business illustrates this perfectly.[7] The chicken's contribution is eggs—a repeatable gift that requires no ultimate sacrifice. The pig, however, offers bacon and sausage, a contribution that demands its very life. Jesus is in the business of changing the world, and He is looking for people who are committed, not just involved.

This commitment is fundamentally expressed through two key implications of the Church being a body, where "every part does its share:"

- **Relationships:** The Church is a body where every joint supplies what is needed. We are knit together by relational connections. This is the heart of true community: deep, meaningful, and often messy relationships that stand in stark contrast to the transactional and superficial ties of the digital age. These are the "circles" that must replace the "rows"—spaces where people can ask honest questions, wrestle with doubt, and build the kind of trust that feels increasingly rare in today's world.

- **Participation:** Every part of the body must do its share. This requires active participation through serving, giving, and sharing our lives with one another. It is the antidote to the consumer-driven mindset that has plagued the modern Church. The younger generation, in particular, is not just looking to belong; they are looking to build.

CULTIVATING A "SECOND TOUCH" OF SPIRITUAL VISION

The story of Jesus healing the blind man in Mark 8 serves as a profound call for the Church to move beyond a "blurry," crowd-centric vision to a "clear," compassionate, and individual-focused approach. The miracle's deliberate two-stage process, rather than an instantaneous healing, teaches us that spiritual growth and the comprehension of profound truths are often incremental journeys, requiring multiple "touches" or encounters with divine revelation. This is a continual process of re-evaluating our vision, confronting our blind spots, and embracing the self-sacrificial, suffering nature of Christ's mission as the ultimate lens through which we see ministry. The Church must move from a blurry vision of a crowd to a clear vision of individuals, fostering genuine belonging by prioritizing relationships over performance.

Cultivating this divine vision requires several core skills:

- **Attentive Listening:** This is paramount for genuine connection. It requires giving full, undivided attention, putting aside distractions, showing genuine interest, and validating another's feelings without judgment or interruption. The biblical injunction to be "quick to listen and slow to speak" (James 1:19) is directly applicable here.

- **Perspective-Taking:** This skill transcends mere agreement; it involves intentionally stepping into someone else's shoes to comprehend their unique experiences and circumstances, even if one does not agree with their choices or actions. It is about "feeling the emotion and stress that the individual's perspective brings."

- **Unconditional Love (Agape):** This is a defining characteristic of perceiving others as God does. By surrendering to the Holy Spirit, believers allow God's limitless and unmatched care to flow through them. This means prioritizing a person's inherent value over the need to be "right" in disagreements.

- **Empathy as a Spiritual Discipline:** True empathy is not merely a psychological skill but a spiritual discipline—a fruit of the Spirit—and a tangible reflection of Christ's character being formed within believers. It involves "spontaneously and naturally tuning into the other person's thoughts and feelings." It is often distinguished into cognitive empathy (recognizing what someone is feeling) and affective empathy (the emotional response that leads to action).

EMBRACING THE MISSION OF "FOR OTHERS"

To honestly answer the belonging question, the Church must embody the radical vision of Bonhoeffer. This means moving from an "attractional" model—which hopes people will come to the church—to a "missional" model, which sends its people and resources out into the world. This outward orientation, focused on serving others within the church and others outside the church, strengthens the internal community and forges deep, resilient bonds among believers. A missional church is deeply present for one another and its community.

The goal is to create a culture of belonging, not just fitting in. "Fitting in" means you are like everyone else. Belonging means you get to be yourself. This is a crucial

THIS IS A PROFOUND CALL FOR THE CHURCH TO MOVE BEYOND A 'BLURRY,' CROWD-CENTRIC VISION TO A 'CLEAR,' COMPASSIONATE, AND INDIVIDUAL-FOCUSED APPROACH.

paradigm shift for congregations. It requires practicing radical hospitality by genuinely welcoming all, especially the marginalized and vulnerable. It means being a church that offers a tangible antidote to loneliness by providing a ready-made social infrastructure grounded in shared values and collective activities. The church, by its very nature, is a spiritual necessity. Its capacity to offer a transcendent framework for identity, purpose, and unconditional acceptance is fundamental to true belonging and to healing the spiritual dimensions of loneliness that pervade modern life.

CREATING SPACES OF ENCOUNTER

The experience of the Corinthian church, as detailed in 1 Corinthians 12-14, offers a robust ancient framework for this modern challenge. The apostle Paul emphasizes that the Church is a unified body with diverse, essential gifts, all given by the same Spirit for the common good. Without love, even the most impressive spiritual gifts are meaningless. When these gifts are used in an orderly, loving way, it creates a powerful environment where even an unbeliever can be convicted and exclaim, "God is really among you!" This passage highlights that the Church, when functioning as intended, becomes a tangible witness to God's reality.

This biblical model is further illuminated by the concept of "Sacred Pathways," which suggests that God designed each person with a unique spiritual temperament. The book *Sacred Pathways* by Gary Thomas argues that authentic worship stems from a connection with God that is aligned with these individual temperaments, freeing people from a one-size-fits-all approach to faith.[8] Some may connect with God through nature, as *Naturalists*, while *Sensates* are drawn to Him through the awe of art and music, and *Intellectuals* engage with God through study and reason. By recognizing these diverse pathways—categorized as Pathways of contemplation, wonder, and action—the Church can create an environment that encourages individuals to be themselves in their relationship with God, fostering a genuine and life-giving connection.

> *FITTING IN* MEANS YOU ARE LIKE EVERYONE ELSE. *BELONGING* MEANS YOU GET TO BE YOURSELF.

The quality of a church community's environment directly influences whether individuals can experience God's presence. A welcoming atmosphere, defined by emotional safety, relational warmth, and peace, can serve as fertile ground for a spiritual encounter, something the chaos of the world seldom allows. While human structures cannot contain or limit God's presence, we are called to intentionally create spaces where people can be transformed by power. This is the kind of church Paul envisioned—one so alive with God's presence that even outsiders recognize it and are compelled to worship.

Cultivating such an environment involves several key elements:
- **Physical Space:** The physical setting should be clean, well-maintained, and aesthetically thoughtful to communicate a sense of value and sacredness.

- **Inclusive Worship:** Worship styles should be understandable and allow for authentic participation, so people can connect with God and the community without feeling like outsiders.

- **Genuine Relationships:** Most importantly, the community's interactions must be characterized by genuine care and mutual respect, reflecting God's love in a tangible way.

The urgency of this task is magnified by the widespread loneliness and disconnection that plague modern society, a crisis with health consequences as severe as smoking 15 cigarettes a day.[9] Young adults, in particular, report significant feelings of loneliness, and the rise of individualism and social isolation creates a deep yearning for authentic community. The Church, by its very nature, can offer a powerful antidote to this loneliness by providing a ready-made social infrastructure grounded in shared values, rituals, and collective activities. By intentionally creating a place of genuine belonging, the Church can become an irresistible beacon of hope in a world that is desperate for authentic connection.

A LESSON FROM AN ENGLISH BREAKFAST

In the complex and chaotic theatre of the twenty-first century, we are constantly being asked to contribute. Our time, our attention, our resources—they are all commodities in the great global marketplace. But as we have seen through the simple, yet profound, allegory of the English breakfast, not all contributions are created equal. The whole, satisfying cacophony of a morning plate tells a story of two fundamentally different kinds of participation: the continuous, repeatable involvement of the chicken and the singular, ultimate commitment of the pig. The sheer numerical disparity—over a thousand eggs consumed for every single pig's life given—is more than a culinary curiosity; it is a profound illustration of the core tension between casual participation and total dedication.

Today, the Church stands at a critical threshold, faced with the invisible, unspoken invitation to breakfast. We have, in many ways, become proficient at providing eggs. We offer services, events, and programs that are the equivalent of the chicken's low-stakes, repeatable input. In an age of unprecedented digital connectedness, we have made it easier than ever for people to be "involved" from a distance. One can watch a sermon online, listen to a podcast, or engage in a group chat, all without the costly, messy, and vulnerable act of true commitment. We have, perhaps unknowingly, cultivated a culture of transactional Christianity, where the gospel is a product to be consumed and the Church is a service to be utilized. We have settled for a flock of chickens—each offering a small, safe contribution— then wondered why our impact feels insubstantial, lacking the weight and transformational power that only true sacrifice can bring.

The uncomfortable truth is that the missing piece in our spiritual breakfast is the pig. The world, and a generation desperate for authentic connection, isn't just looking for another egg; they are yearning for a community willing to offer its very life. The commitment of the pig—a complete forfeiture for a shared purpose—is the spiritual sacrifice that a consumer-driven culture cannot replicate. It is the difference between watching from the safety of the shore and stepping out onto the stormy water. It is the willingness to be bruised and broken, to get messy and vulnerable, to give up control and lay down one's life for the sake of the mission. This is the costly, non-renewable contribution that builds trust, forges deep relationships, and creates a community that is truly transformative.

To move forward, we must stop settling for involvement and become radically committed. We must cultivate a culture where dedication is celebrated and sacrifice is seen not as a loss, but as the very essence of discipleship. This means challenging ourselves and our communities to become more than a collection of individuals offering eggs. It means becoming a people willing to give our bacon—our entire selves—for the sake of the gospel. It is a call to move from transactional contributions to transformational commitment. It is time to truly step out of the boat and into the messy, sacred work of building a church that is less about billions of eggs and more about the ultimate sacrifice that changes everything.

HE IS LOOKING
FOR PEOPLE WHO
ARE *COMMITTED*,
NOT JUST *INVOLVED*.

CHAPTER 8 SUMMARY

This chapter frames the Church's historical role as a "third place"—a neutral ground for community and belonging—and laments its shift toward becoming an "entertainment venue" or "information service." It identifies a global epidemic of loneliness and a deep human yearning for belonging that the Church is uniquely positioned to answer. The chapter asserts that the Church is not an institution but a "people together as His body for others" and must move from viewing congregants as a dehumanized crowd to seeing them as unique individuals. It introduces the metaphor of the chicken and the pig to distinguish between casual involvement and total commitment, arguing that true belonging is found in a committed community willing to give its life for a shared purpose, not just its eggs.

SKILL:
ENGAGE ALL WITH INSIGHT & COLLABORATIVE LEADERSHIP

REFLECTIVE QUESTIONS

1. How are you intentionally building an intergenerational community?

2. How is your ministry addressing the loneliness epidemic, especially among youth?

3. How can your church shift from platform-focused to presence-focused ministry?

JOIN THE CONVERSATION
& WATCH THE INTERVIEWS HERE

CONCLUSION

GOD IS IN OUR FUTURE

SUCCESS IS FAR
MORE DANGEROUS
THAN *FAILURE* BECAUSE
SUCCESS CAUSES YOU
TO *DO* IT AGAIN,
WHILE FAILURE CAUSES
YOU TO *TRY* AGAIN.

CHAPTER 9

TOWARD 2050

The story is well-known, almost a cliché of scientific discovery. In 1928, a Scottish microbiologist named Alexander Fleming returned to his lab after a two-week vacation to find a mess. Petri dishes, left in a stack on his bench, were contaminated.[1] A lesser scientist might have simply thrown them all away, but Fleming, with a particular kind of intellectual sloppiness, paused. He noticed something odd in one of the dishes containing Staphylococcus bacteria.[1] A patch of mold had grown, and all around it, in a perfect, bacteria-free halo, the colonies had vanished.

This wasn't a discovery. Not yet. It was an anomaly. An accident. A beautiful, serendipitous mistake born from careless lab practices. But what Fleming did next— with keen observation and subsequent investigation—was what turned an accident into a breakthrough. He didn't dismiss the error; he leaned into it. He isolated the mold, identified it as Penicillium notatum, and, through persistent experimentation, realized it produced a substance that killed bacteria.[1] The world would later know this substance as penicillin, one of the most important medical discoveries in human history.[1]

Fleming's messy lab and his subsequent discovery are not merely a tale of good fortune. They are a profound parable for the future of the Church. For too long, many of us have operated like meticulous, well-organized scientists, perfectly following a plan. We've thrown out the "contaminated" dishes, the failed programs, and the unexpected results, all in the name of efficiency and control. But in doing so, have we been missing the halo, the unexpected sign, the very thing God might be doing right outside the bounds of our carefully designed experiments?

What Fleming's story illustrates is not a lesson in how to get lucky, but a lesson in what we call the "lab mentality." This mindset is a commitment to continuous inquiry and experimentation, where a failed test is not a dead end but a new data point. It's a culture that actively encourages us to try new things and, most importantly, to learn from what doesn't work. This is not about being reckless; it is a disciplined approach to turning ideas into actionable processes.

A lab mentality is built on the principles of agile adaptation,[2] a framework for navigating uncertainty that has transformed everything from software development to rocket science. At its core, it emphasizes:

- **Curiosity and Hypothesis Testing:** Instead of assuming we have all the answers, we start with provocative questions and structure our ideas into testable hypotheses. We ask, *"What if we tried this?"*—then we methodically investigate the outcome, moving from presumed knowledge to evidence-based approaches.

- **Learning from Failure:** Mistakes and unexpected results are not setbacks but invaluable data points for growth. This creates a psychologically safe space where we can try new things without fear of punishment, and it's what allows for the continuous improvement that is vital in a world changing at an exponential rate.

- **Data-Driven Iteration:** We use feedback loops to measure progress, not just in terms of output, but in terms of validated learning. This rigorous, scientific method helps us determine whether to pivot (change course) or persevere (continue with our current approach) based on what we learn.

Just as the accidental observation of a fuzzy mold led to a medical revolution, so too can the unexpected outcomes of our ministry experiments—the programs that didn't work, the outreach that fell flat, the sermon that landed on deaf ears—contain the seeds of our next significant breakthrough. The future of faith, it turns out, might be found not in the polished perfection of a well-executed plan, but in the humble, messy, and courageous posture of a living laboratory.

THE FUTURE OF *FAITH*, IT TURNS OUT, MIGHT BE FOUND NOT IN THE POLISHED PERFECTION OF A WELL-EXECUTED PLAN, BUT IN THE *HUMBLE*, *MESSY*, AND *COURAGEOUS* POSTURE OF A LIVING LABORATORY.

This lab mentality is crucial because, as Terry Parkman, a key global voice for the next generation, observes, the Church must stop thinking "attractionally and start thinking adaptively." We cannot see the future through a church lens alone; we must look holistically—rooted in scripture, in history, and in precedent—so we can build what's next from a solid foundation. Our world is undergoing a "world-historic change" driven by interconnected technological tipping points like AI, clean energy, and bioengineering. These are not isolated phenomena, but foundational shifts that demand a new kind of response from the Church.

Our approach to this must be rooted in a deep-seated understanding of how change works. We have learned that change is the process through which the future invades our lives. It's an ever-present reality that impacts individuals and organizations, and our ability to navigate it effectively depends on understanding its catalysts: crisis, disruption, innovation, and obedience. By recognizing these forces, we can move from being passive victims to active agents of change, shaping a future that aligns with our highest values and deepest hopes.

Consider a common idiom that highlights different levels of strategic thinking: "She was playing chess while he was playing checkers." This phrase vividly illustrates a disparity in foresight and planning. Checkers is a game of simple, often direct moves, where pieces follow predictable paths and individual actions are mainly independent. Chess, on the other hand, demands a far more profound understanding of interconnectedness, anticipating multiple moves ahead, sacrificing pieces for long-term gain, and understanding the intricate consequences of each decision. When applied to leadership or organizational strategy, it suggests that one party is operating with a limited, short-sighted view, while the other is engaging with a more sophisticated, holistic, and long-term perspective, understanding the broader system and anticipating future challenges and opportunities.

In a world often content with playing checkers, the Church is called to play Jenga. Checkers is about isolated pieces moving across a flat board; Jenga is about intricate, layered stability where every block depends on the ones beneath it. This difference highlights a crucial reality for the future of faith: true collaboration, genuine community, and effective teamwork are not about superficial alliances, but about building on deep, unwavering foundations.

Our *Jenga* tower of collaboration, as we've explored throughout this book, stands on three interconnected blocks: truth, trust, and teamwork. Crucially, one builds upon the other, and the entire structure is only as firm as its base. If the foundation is unstable, the whole thing falls apart. Truth forms the base— the most critical layer of all. Upon truth, trust can be built. And only on the solid ground of trust can we engage in the kind of effective teamwork that truly advances the gospel.

FOUNDATIONS OF HEALTHY TEAMWORK

TEAMWORK

TRUST

TRUTH

In many of our societies today, there's a pervasive tendency to shy away from uncomfortable truths. We've become adept at political correctness, carefully curating our words to avoid offense, often at the cost of genuine understanding. But political correctness is not the same as truth. In our attempts to be perpetually agreeable, we frequently prevent the very conversations necessary to build the foundational block of truth. When we cannot speak honestly about our differences, our historical wounds, or our genuine experiences, we are left with shallow connections incapable of bearing the weight of true collaboration.

Consider the profound example of the South African Truth and Reconciliation Commission (TRC) in the post-apartheid era.[3] Faced with centuries of brutal racial hatred and division, Bishop Desmond Tutu and Nelson Mandela championed a radical path: a public, televised court where perpetrators of horrific crimes could confess their actions, and victims or their families could offer forgiveness. This was not about punishment; it was about revealing the brutal facts. People stood up and said, "I killed your father because he was of a different race than me. Will you forgive me?" And in those raw, televised moments, amidst tears and pain, truth brought forth a possibility of reconciliation.

The TRC demonstrated a powerful, uncomfortable truth: there is no reconciliation without truth. As the saying goes, we can only hate that which we do not know. When we refuse to engage with the difficult truths of our collective past or present, when we sanitize our conversations for the sake of artificial harmony, we perpetuate misunderstanding and distrust. Even when we disagree entirely with someone, understanding their "why" and gaining insight moves us from hatred to pity. No amount of understanding why will justify their actions, but understanding why lays the groundwork for empathy.

THERE IS NO *RECONCILIATION* WITHOUT *TRUTH*.

This empathy, born from truth, is what enables us to move past hatred and toward the possibility of trust. Our politically correct carefulness often precludes us from authentic, deep relationships because we never have truth, and therefore we don't build trust, and thus, we can never truly be in deep, transformative relationships together.

Only when the truth is bravely faced and openly acknowledged can the second block—trust—begins to form. Trust isn't built on platitudes or superficial pleasantries; it's forged in the crucible of shared reality, even if that reality is painful. It requires vulnerability—the courage to overcome our fear of rejection by allowing others to cover our weaknesses and contribute to our strengths. When we understand someone's story, their intentions, and their struggles, we can begin to trust them, even if their actions initially seemed incomprehensible. As Nicole Martin shares, the Truth is infallible, but we are not, and our credibility grows when we are willing to say, "*I got that wrong.*"

And once truth creates the foundation for trust, the final block—teamwork—becomes not only possible, but powerfully practical. This is where the extraordinary amplification effect of collaboration comes into play. Think back to the draft horses: when they're trained to work together, leaning on each other's strengths, two can do the work of four. Our collective ability to change the world for Christ, to address the urgent challenges facing the next generation, is amplified exponentially when we work together with other individuals, other teams, and other organizations within the Kingdom of God.

The strategic moves required to play *Jenga* often demand a posture of listening and obedience, especially when the path is unclear. The future of the Church may well hinge on our ability to play *Jenga* in a checkers world. It demands that we prioritize truth over comfort, cultivate trust through honest engagement, and then leverage the immense power of genuine teamwork to advance the gospel. It's a simple, yet profoundly challenging, blueprint for building a thriving church that can truly change the world.

KNOWING WHAT TO KEEP AND WHAT TO RISK

To truly lead in this new era, we must develop a profound sense of discernment—the ability to know what must be held as sacred and unchanging, and what must be risked for the sake of the mission. Our core mission, the gospel, remains as potent as ever. Our challenge lies not in the message, but in our methods. These are simply tools to serve a greater purpose and must never be held as sacred. This calls for a delicate, Spirit-led discernment: to preserve what must be protected and risk what must be released.

Consider the metaphor of a golf swing. For a seasoned golfer, the swing is a complex, fluid motion refined over the years. Trying to fix one small element can throw the entire kinetic chain out of sync, leading to a complete breakdown of the swing. The result is often worse than the original problem, a frustrating reminder that a minor change can have a major, and sometimes negative, impact. In the same way, leaders often face the temptation to either cling tightly to the past or discard it entirely in a frantic pursuit of relevance. The wise leader understands that a small change can make a big difference, but they also know that not every change is for the best. To discern the difference, we must learn the art of the second touch.

As mentioned before, the story of Jesus healing the blind man in Mark 8 is a powerful illustration of this. Jesus' first touch gave the man partial vision, allowing him to see people as if they were trees walking. His vision was blurry, but it was a start. He could see, but not with perfect clarity. It was only after a second touch that the man's sight was fully restored. This intentional, two-step process reminds us that spiritual growth—and the grasping of deeper truths—unfolds gradually, over time, not in a single moment. Our leadership in this season requires the same patience and intentionality. We must be willing to apply a second touch, seeking clarity and refinement rather than a complete overhaul. This requires a willingness to break something—not for the sake of disruption, but for the sake of improvement. It's the courage to dismantle outdated methods or systems because we believe they can be rebuilt to serve a greater purpose. We're not breaking just to break—we're breaking with a clear and compelling vision of a better future.

To do this effectively, we must:

• **Keep the main thing the main thing.** As we refine our methods, our compass must remain fixed on our true north. Our unchanging mission, anchored in the gospel, is the constant amidst all the currents of change. As Vince Parker reminds us, we stand on the cross, and that is enough.

• **Seek outside perspective**. Like a golfer needing a coach to diagnose a flawed swing, we must seek the unvarnished truth from outside our echo chambers. This is the role of the global conversations that inform this book—providing an external, prophetic perspective on the shifts that are often invisible to us from the inside.

- **Keep trying until it is better.** Thomas Edison's journey to the lightbulb, which involved thousands of unsuccessful attempts, is a powerful reminder that innovation is a process of relentless iteration. We must cultivate an experimental mentality, willing to try new things, learn from what doesn't work, and adjust our course until we find what does.

This is the art of leadership in a world of accelerating change. It is not about reckless innovation or fearful preservation. It is about the discerning, humble work of a second touch—retaining the core and refining the form, so that the power of the gospel can be delivered with perfect clarity and impact.

This is a form of innovation—a strategic process for implementing change to advance the gospel. To do so, we must be willing to both start new things and stop old ones. We must embrace the art of innovation on both an individual and corporate level, recognizing that sometimes we must lay down what brought us success in the past to achieve success in the future.

THE ART OF INNOVATION

Innovation isn't merely about adopting the latest technology; it's a strategic process for implementing change to advance the gospel. The *Art of Innovation* is the methodology for the pioneer, requiring a critical evaluation of existing practices and the introduction of new approaches that strengthen human relationships with God. It is not a skill reserved for a select few but a discipline for every leader and organization seeking to remain relevant in a world of rapid change. Just as pioneers venture into uncharted territory, innovation is the process of navigating the unknown, intentionally moving beyond yesterday's methods to align with the unchanging mission of God.

THE ART OF INNOVATION
CHANGE IS THE WAY THE FUTURE INVADES THE PRESENT

	STOP	START
INDIVIDUAL	**TERMINATION** THE HORSE IS DEAD	**ILLUMINATION** CHANGE YOUR ANGLE
CORPORATE	**SIMPLIFICATION** LESS IS MORE	**COLLABORATION** BETTER TOGETHER

To effectively innovate, we must be willing to both start new things and stop old ones. This requires a balance of individual and corporate effort. As you consider how to apply this in your context, think about these four quadrants of innovation:

- **Termination:** Recognizing when a method is no longer effective. This is the individual act of stopping things that no longer serve the mission, a task often as tricky as starting something new. We must be humble enough to admit that what brought us success in the past might not lead to success in the future. This requires us to lay down outdated methods for the sake of the mission. The horse is dead—stop hitting it—a powerful reminder to let go of practices that have lost their purpose. A pioneer knows when to leave behind old maps and canoes when they encounter mountains they are unprepared for.

- **Simplification:** Doing less to do more. On a corporate level, this means stopping the proliferation of programs and initiatives that can overwhelm an organization. Many organizations fail not from doing too little, but from trying to do too much. Simplifying our efforts allows us to focus on what truly matters and to do one thing well rather than failing at everything. Simplification is the discipline of doing less to do more, allowing the pioneer to focus their energy on what truly matters.

- **Illumination:** Gaining a new perspective. As individuals, we must intentionally seek exposure to new ideas and perspectives. This involves stepping outside of our comfort zones to encounter new people and new ideas that can provide a new angle or a different perspective. Illumination is the pioneer's commitment to constantly seeking new perspectives and ideas, reading trends and evaluating trajectories. This is how they "see" the ball they cannot see.

- **Collaboration:** Working together for a greater impact. The future of faith is not a solitary journey. Collaboration is essential for moving forward, and we must find ways to work together as a community, sharing ideas and resources. This is about acknowledging that we are better together and that our collective effort can achieve far more than any one of us could alone. Collaboration is the pioneer's recognition that they are better together, leveraging shared strength to do what no one could achieve on their own.

FIVE GUIDING PRINCIPLES FOR INNOVATION

To cultivate a mindset of innovation, consider these five principles that can help you and your organization navigate change effectively:

1. **See the Big Picture:** Stay up to date on current trends and how they impact the church and community. This is about looking beyond your immediate context to understand the broader forces at play.

2. **Keep Trying and Testing:** Adopt an experimental mindset to test new ideas and approaches without fear of failure. This is about developing a lab mentality where setbacks are seen not as failures, but as valuable learning opportunities. Success is far more dangerous than failure because success causes you to do it again, while failure causes you to try again.

3. **Think Inside the Box:** Leverage existing church strengths, resources, and capabilities in innovative ways. This is about recognizing the immense value of what you already have and finding creative ways to apply it to new challenges. You don't always need to invent something entirely new; sometimes the most impactful innovation is a new application of an old strength.

4. **Good Enough Is Good Enough:** Value openness and learning over fixed mindsets and assumptions. Innovation doesn't require perfection to be implemented. We must be willing to release things into the world before they are perfectly formed, learning and adapting along the way. The pursuit of perfection can often be a form of stagnation, preventing us from moving forward at all.

5. **Major on the Majors:** Focus on the core mission and values rather than getting distracted. Innovation should always serve the gospel, not be pursued for its own sake. The purpose is to connect people with a life-changing relationship with the living God. Our purpose remains what it has always been, and our methods should always serve this unchanging mission.

Ultimately, the Art of Innovation is a journey of discernment and courage. It's about being willing to let go of old practices that no longer serve their purpose. It's about embracing the power of collaboration and working together as a community. And it's about staying informed and embracing the future with hope, knowing that innovation is an ongoing process that allows us to navigate the challenges and opportunities ahead.

The pioneer spirit, introduced at the beginning of this book, is the "why" behind this journey—the courage to venture into the unknown rather than settle for a "mathematical technicality." The Art of Innovation is the "how," providing the strategic framework for the pioneer to move forward. The pioneer has the courage to break free from the familiar, and the innovator has the methodology to build something new from the broken pieces. This is a crucial distinction: one is a posture of the heart, while the other is a discipline of the hand. Both are essential for accelerating the gospel into the future.

BEATING THE GAME

In the world of classic video games, there are few stories as compelling as that of a 13-year-old from Oklahoma who, in December 2023, accomplished the impossible: he beat the 1986 Nintendo Entertainment System (NES) version of Tetris, a game designed to be endless.[4] Known as "Blue Scuti," Willis Gibson's victory was not merely a personal triumph but a culmination of a living tradition. It was an achievement that echoed the spirit of pioneers and revealed three key lessons for those of us striving to accelerate Christianity into the future.

1. Working with Technology to See What's Possible
For decades, the "kill screen" of Tetris was considered the final, unbeatable frontier for human players. The pieces simply fell too fast to be managed. But in 2021, an AI program played the game to a point where the speed became so extreme that it crashed,[5] showing the human community what was on the other side of the impossible level and revealing that victory was, in fact, possible.

This is a powerful illustration of the book's central message: technology is a neutral tool, and its impact is determined by our intent and our skill in using it.

Like the AI that showed a way forward in Tetris, technological advancements—from AI and social media to biotechnology—are not the enemy. They are catalysts that, when used with wisdom, can reveal new possibilities and expand the reach of our human capabilities and spiritual mission. The Church must stop being afraid of these tools and, instead, learn to leverage them to see a future for the gospel that was previously unimaginable.

2. A Call to Community and Collaboration

Willis Gibson did not accomplish this feat in isolation. He was part of a thriving "living tradition" of players, streamers, bloggers, and theorists who were all trying to outmatch one another and push the game to its limits. This community was a *living laboratory of ideas and experimentation* where new techniques and strategies were tested and shared. The "rolling" technique, which allowed players to input commands faster than ever before, was a direct product of this communal innovation, and it was instrumental in Gibson's success.

This directly mirrors our call for a Church that is a community of collaboration, not just a crowd of consumers. The future of faith won't be shaped by isolated heroes but by a collective, collaborative body that shares knowledge, resources, and a vision for the future. As with the Tetris community, we are better together. We must move beyond the illusion of connection fostered by digital platforms and create genuine, in-person communities where people can learn, grow, and tackle challenges together. This is especially critical in a world marked by a redefinition of connectedness, where we have many online "friends" but few real ones. The digital age, with its AI companions and virtual interactions, can lead to a state of curated loneliness. To counter this, the Church must shift from "rows" to "circles," creating spaces where people can ask difficult questions, wrestle with doubt, and build authentic relationships. Young people are looking for a community that is willing to give its "bacon"—its entire self, not just its "eggs" of casual involvement.

PROFOUND, GAME-CHANGING ACHIEVEMENTS REQUIRE MORE THAN JUST A PASSING INTEREST; THEY DEMAND *LONG OBEDIENCE* IN THE *SAME DIRECTION*.

3. The Power of Grit and Long Obedience

Gibson's famous 38-minute winning run was the direct result of thousands of hours of preparation and a deep dedication to his craft. In a world of short attention spans and fleeting trends, his success is a testament to the power of grit and long-haul commitment. Profound, game-changing achievements require more than just a passing interest; they demand long obedience in the same direction.

As we seek to "hit the ball we cannot see," we too must cultivate the resilience and determination to keep our eyes on the prize, trusting that our dedication, even when the pace feels relentless, is essential. We must be like the pioneers who, with unwavering conviction, dared to venture into the unknown. Our faithfulness is not measured by our ability to keep up with every trend but by our ability to remain in step with the Spirit as we steward our mission over the long haul.

This is our hopeful prediction. Just as a teenager, fueled by innovation and community, proved that the impossible could be beaten, we too can rise to the challenges of our time. By working with technology, fostering authentic community, and committing to the long obedience required, we can move from being overwhelmed by the game to collectively winning it. We can, and we will, continue to advance the gospel into a future that is bright, filled with hope, and ultimately anchored in the unwavering presence of God.

This long obedience is not about frantic action, but about aligning ourselves with God's rhythm. As Lisa Pak reminds us, "Jesus was urgent, yes, but never rushed." We need to marry our urgency to reach the world with discernment, ensuring our strategies are not just timely but also deeply rooted in God's pace. This is the spirit of a pioneer—not someone who rushes headlong into the unknown, but someone who, with a compass and a clear sense of purpose, deliberately charts a course through unpredictable waters.

GOD IS IN OUR FUTURE

Ephesians 2:10 states, "For we are God's handiwork, created in Christ Jesus to do good works, which God prepared in advance for us to do" (NIV). Despite the evolving world around us, God is present in the future we are heading toward. This powerful truth changes everything. It means that while the future may be unknown to us, it is not unknown to God. He is not reacting to the chaos; He is already present within it, preparing good works for us to walk into.

This divine foresight provides the ultimate anchor in a world of constant motion. The fastballs of technology, social shifts, and cultural fragmentation may feel faster than we can see, but our mission is not to hit a ball we cannot see on our own. Our task is to align ourselves with the One who has already prepared the way, swinging our bat not out of a frantic reaction, but out of faithful anticipation.

This should influence our approach to innovation and change. We're not just adjusting to stay current with trends like the Joneses or Zuckerbergs; we're aligning ourselves with God's continuous work in the world as if we are collaborators with Him in crafting the next chapter of His narrative on Earth. Our faith doesn't lie in our capacity to foresee or manage what's to come. We are dedicated to nurturing believers who authentically embody their faith in a world of deep complexity. It may seem unconventional, but remember, when Jesus first introduced the concept of the "Kingdom of God," many likely found it just as surprising.

The ultimate conclusion of this book is both simple and challenging. We must recognize that the world is changing. As pioneers, we must be willing to leave behind the comfort of the familiar and adapt our methods to remain relevant. This means shedding the fluff that obscures the gospel and embracing new forms of community, collaboration, and discipleship. We must also understand that God is constant and eternally relevant. His truth is our immovable anchor, and we don't need to invent a new gospel, but rather, present the ancient one with humble, human clarity. Finally, we need to keep our eyes on Him. Our role is to faithfully follow His leading, seeking His wisdom and guidance as we navigate the challenges and opportunities of our time.

By aligning ourselves with His purposes, we can trust that He will empower us to fulfil His mission. The future is bright because Christ Himself is building His Church. He loves every person, in every place, to the ends of the earth—far more than we ever could. Our role is to continue innovating—not for the sake of being trendy, but to faithfully and effectively walk in the good works He has already prepared for us. As we do so, we can be confident that the mission will not fail, for we serve a God who is already in all of time, all the time.

CHAPTER 9 SUMMARY

This concluding chapter offers a hopeful vision for the future of faith, framed by the parable of Alexander Fleming's penicillin discovery, which illustrates the importance of a "lab mentality"—a commitment to continuous experimentation and learning from unexpected results. It challenges the Church to stop playing checkers and instead play *Jenga* by building on the foundational blocks of truth, trust, and teamwork. The chapter introduces the *Art of Innovation* as a discipline for every leader, involving the four quadrants of termination, simplification, illumination, and collaboration. It concludes with the story of a teenager beating Tetris, highlighting the power of leveraging technology, fostering community, and committing to "long obedience in the same direction" to achieve what was once thought impossible. Finally, we conclude with this reminder: rest in the hope that God is already present in our future.

REFLECTIVE QUESTIONS

1. What legacy are you building toward 2050—and what will need to be let go in order to get there?

2. Who in the next generation are you walking with into the future of faith?

3. What is one "impossible" thing you sense God calling you to pioneer in this season?

JOIN THE CONVERSATION
& WATCH THE INTERVIEWS HERE

OUR MISSION IS NOT TO
HIT A BALL WE CANNOT
SEE ON OUR *OWN*.
OUR TASK IS TO *ALIGN*
OURSELVES WITH
THE *ONE* WHO HAS
ALREADY PREPARED
THE WAY.

SHIFTS, IMPACT & SKILLS
SUMMARY

CHANGE IN	CHAPTER TITLE	SHIFT	IMPACT	SKILL
HOW WE LIVE	SHIFTING DEFINITION OF BEING HUMAN	Technology and social movements are changing the very definition of what it means to be human.	This disorientation creates an identity crisis, making outdated methodologies feel archaic and irrelevant.	Provide clear, foundational truths about our identity in Christ without needing to answer every question. Clarity over certainty.
	SHIFTING DELINEATIONS OF DIGITAL EXISTENCE	Our digital existence is the norm, reshaping reality, identity, and our perception of truth.	Genuine human interaction becomes scarce, creating a fragmented self and intense competition for our focused attention.	Leverage high-tech to connect, and prioritize authentic human relationships and meaningful, high-touch spiritual experiences.
HOW THE WORLD WORKS	SHIFTING DYNAMICS OF TRUST	Society has polarized, moving from shared consensus to extreme division, causing a total collapse of trust.	This pervasive mistrust erodes values and perceived value, making it difficult to accept the Church's truth.	In a polarized world, build relational credibility through presence and transparency before presenting the truth.
	SHIFTING DIMENSIONS OF ORGANIZATION	Wealth gaps, automation, and self-sufficiency are causing old organizational structures and models to completely unravel.	This can lead to a disconnected, consumer-driven church that struggles to foster collaborative and interdependent leadership.	Shift from a top-down model by equipping and empowering others with resources, responsibility, and authority.
HOW WE CONNECT	SHIFTING DEGREES OF SEPARATION	Technology collapses distances but fuels a hyper-individualized post-community society that leaves people more isolated than ever.	Disconnection and loneliness cause a generation to mistrust Christian institutions, which often mirrors the world's fragmentation.	Counteract individualism by fostering radical collaboration and unity around a shared mission bigger than any individual.
	SHIFTING DISCOVERY OF BELONGING	The decline of community "third places" has intensified a global loneliness epidemic and an unmet need to belong.	A consumer-driven church offers passive involvement instead of the radical commitment required for true, missional belonging.	Move people from passive consumption to active, committed participation in a truly collaborative and missional community.

CONTRIBUTORS

Though the content of this book was informed by several research projects, documents, conferences and conversations and insights from the whole of the NXT Move community these individuals contributed by specifically being interviewed or contributed in writing towards it.

ANIA GREENWOOD

STEIGER.ORG

Ania Greenwood is a creative evangelist, missionary and leader of Steiger Poland. Serving with Steiger since 2004, she has ministered in England, Brazil, and, for the past eight years, in Poland, where she develops urban mission teams and inspires creative outreach across Europe. Based in Wrocław with her husband and two children, Ania is launching a Cultural and Mission Center that will unite innovative evangelism, the arts, and business-in-mission. She leads projects such as Revolutionary Art, I Am, and KIMJESTEM.ART, engaging the Global Youth Culture with the message of Jesus in relevant and creative ways.

For the past few years she has led international missions trips to one of the largest festivals in Europe, *Pol&Rock,* boldly and relevantly sharing the gospel with thousands. Passionate and visionary, she consistently inspires others, fuels creativity, and builds bridges between the Church and today's Global Youth Culture.

BOSHOFF GROBLER

Boshoff Grobler is a seasoned entrepreneur, executive leader, and transformational coach with over two decades of experience spanning investment banking, asset management, social enterprise, and spiritual leadership.

He played a key role in founding several high-impact ventures within Africa's largest financial services group, including Ashburton Investments, and Rand Merchant Bank's Debt Capital Markets unit.

His leadership extends beyond finance into purpose-driven innovation. As co-founder of Phahama Lodge and The Adventure Institute, Boshoff has championed job creation and leadership development in South Africa's outdoor adventure sector. He also chairs several non-profits focused on ethical leadership and youth empowerment, including Unashamedly Ethical and NXTMove.

Boshoff holds a BCom (Law) and LLB from the University of Pretoria, an LLM in Banking and Corporate Law from the University of Johannesburg, and an Executive Master in Change from INSEAD.

His leadership is deeply rooted in his Christian faith, guided by values of justice, truth, and transformation.

DAN BLYTHE

@ALPHAYTH @DANBLYTHE8
ALPHA.ORG/YOUTH

Dan serves as the Global Youth Director for Alpha, collaborating with both young individuals and youth leaders to ignite inspiration, foster innovation, and provide unwavering support for Alpha's mission to spread the gospel among young people on a global scale. Dan has been involved in youth ministry for over 20 years and loves every minute of it.

Dan has been married to his wife, Charlie, for 15 years and they have two boys, Knox (age 6) and Niko (age 3), who they are raising to support Chelsea FC.

JENNIFER BROWN

Jenn Brown serves as Vice President of Collaborative Partnerships at OneHope. In her role, she works to build strategic partnerships and foster Kingdom collaborations to reach the next generation globally. In addition to her role with OneHope, Jenn serves as Executive Director of Propel Women, through which she aims to activate women to follow Jesus wholeheartedly as they lead in their workplaces, homes, and communities. Jenn holds a Doctor of Ministry in Missiology from Southeastern University.

She lives in sunny South Florida with her mini golden doodle, River.

JIYOUNG YOO

Jiyoung Yoo is the CEO of With Jesus Publishing and KnotsLab, Christian publishing houses in South Korea dedicated to producing Christ-centered resources that inspire spiritual growth and global mission. She also serves with With Jesus Ministry, where she equips and encourages believers to cultivate a deeper, more intimate walk with Jesus Christ.

In global ministry, Jiyoung is a leader within the Lausanne Movement's Bridge Leader Initiative and serves as secretary for Korea's Lausanne Younger Leaders Generation. Her work is fueled by a passion for connecting people, vision, and ministries across cultures for the advancement of God's kingdom. She is committed to creating Christ-centered communities of leaders so that they can finish their journey and calling well.

Before stepping into publishing and ministry leadership, Jiyoung built a career in media as a journalist and television writer in both the United States and South Korea. This unique background enables her to bridge cultures, communicate with clarity, and bring stories to life in ways that resonate with younger Christian audiences.

Jiyoung's life mission is to see leaders encouraged, united, and equipped to run with perseverance—and to finish well for the glory of God.

KEVIN LEE

KEVIN.LEE@PURPOSEACCELERATOR.ORG
PURPOSEACCELERATOR.ORG

Kevin is a leading China Marketing Strategist and Consumer-centric Innovation Expert. As Founding Partner at China Youthology, a leading consumer insights & innovation consultancy, he has served 15 years as a senior consultant for executives at many of the leading Fortune 500.

Kevin has been coaching individuals to discover their identity and purpose for over 20 years. 10 years ago, Kevin embarked on a research study to uncover what are the key personal traits needed to thrive in our hyper-changing world, and the developmental triggers that produce those traits.

Today, Kevin is Founder of the Purpose Accelerator, a program that helps individuals discover their personal purpose. Through this interactive course of lectures, workshops, activities and coaching, individuals find a structured way of making progress in discovering themselves and their life's calling.

Kevin is a highly demanded public speaker, frequently speaking at international summits like the Microsoft CEO Summit, Cannes Lions International Festival of Creativity, Consumer Goods Forum Global Summit, DLD, and many more.

Kevin is a Goalkeeper, in association with the Bill & Melinda Gates Foundation, a native Canadian, who lived in China for 20 years, and a graduate of Schulich School of Business, York University, receiving an MBA with dean's list honors.

KRISTEN SHULER

EASTWEST.ORG

Kristen's life has been shaped by a core passion: to see the gospel transform communities worldwide. As President of East-West, Kristen provides strategic leadership and directs the ministry's daily operations. She unifies the efforts of the field ministry, support operations, and development teams, while forging key external partnerships to advance the organization's mission.

A veteran leader within the organization, Kristen has been instrumental in its growth since 2010, previously serving as Executive Vice President of Development and Senior Vice President of Field Leadership. Her leadership is built on a foundation of hands-on field experience with the International Mission Board, where she developed and implemented evangelism and church planting strategies across South America. This deep-rooted passion for missions continues to be the driving force behind her work.

Kristen is married to Micah, and they are proud parents to three daughters: Olive, Ivy, and Eve.

LISA PAK

Reverend Dr. Lisa Pak is a second-generation Korean Canadian and Toronto native. She currently serves as the Director of Partnerships (Asia) alongside Rick Warren at Finishing the Task (FTT), in addition to focusing on collaborative efforts toward empowering women and the rising generations for kingdom purpose. She also serves with Wycliffe USA in collaborative strategy and prayer. She previously served as the Regional Director for Ontario and Nunavut at the Canadian Bible Society, and spent over a decade in pastoral ministry within the Korean Church communities throughout the the United States, South Korea, Singapore, and Canada. She is ordained by the Korean Association of Independent Churches and Missions (KAICAM). She holds an Honours BA in Philosophy and Religion from the University of Toronto, a Master of Divinity and a Master of Arts in Biblical Languages from Gordon-Conwell Theological Seminary, and has also earned her Doctor of Ministry in Leadership from Tyndale Seminary.

Lisa travels globally and is passionate about mobilizing the global Church, especially the rising generations, toward collaboration in sharing the good news of Jesus Christ with all who have yet to hear. She also enjoys teaching, loves animals, and her favorite movie is "Gladiator."

LUKE GREENWOOD

Luke Greenwood is passionate about evangelism and discipleship among alternative scenes of the Global Youth Culture. He currently lives in Wrocław, Poland with his wife Ania and two children.

As Steiger Europe Director, Luke's vision is to see Jesus proclaimed to young people all over the continent, and to establish dynamic, long-term City Teams in key urban centers, that reach and equip the Global Youth Culture through creative evangelism, ongoing discipleship, and local church partnership. Together with the Steiger Europe team, Luke has helped develop such actions in over 30 cities across Europe in the past 5 years, and prays for teams reaching secular culture in every major European city.

In 2019, Luke authored the book, *Global Youth Culture: The Spiritual Hunger of the Largest Unreached Culture Today.* He is the frontman and singer of the evangelistic band The Unrest.

Luke often shares the vision of Steiger in churches and conferences, and teaches annually at the Steiger Missions School in Krögis, Germany, on the topics of Evangelism and Discipleship to the Global Youth Culture.

Previously, Luke worked with Steiger Brazil, leading Alegorica, a Brazilian version of the No Longer Music show. He also led the community house Espaço Coletivo and a movement of evangelistic art and music events called Manifeste.

Luke loves to challenge people to live lives of radical faith and to courageously engage the Global Youth Culture with the Gospel.

MATTHEW NIERMANN

MATTHEWNIERMANN.COM

Rev. Dr. Matthew Niermann serves as the Director of Global Research for the Lausanne Movement. In addition, he currently serves as the Director of the Institute of Great Commission Research at California Baptist University, and the Director of the Center for Creativity and Christian Witness at the College of Architecture, Visual Arts, and Design where he also serves as Professor of Architectural Design. Matthew has earned a Ph.D. in Architectural Design from the University of Michigan and an M.A. in Apologetics from Biola University, an M.A. in Theology, and a Th.M. in Missiology from Gordon-Conwell Theological Seminary.

MICHAEL A. ORTIZ

@ MICHAEL A. ORTIZ
@MICHAEL_ORTIZ
ICETE.INFO
DTS.EDU

Dr. Michael A. Ortiz serves as Executive Director for the International Council for Evangelical Theological Education.

Michael was born in New York City to Cuban immigrants. After receiving a law degree from Southern Methodist University in 1988 and developing his practice in Florida, he submitted his life to Christ. In 2015, he received his PhD in Theological Education from Seminario Teológico Centroamericano (SETECA) following his ThM in New Testament from Dallas Theological Seminary in 2008.

He also serves as Vice President for Global Ministries and is a Professor of Missiology and Intercultural Ministries at Dallas Theological Seminary. He oversees the Seminary's language programs (Chinese, Spanish, and Arabic), free online programs, international student development and discipleship, research on global pastoral training, and the worldwide training of pastoral leaders through DTS.

He's been married to Kathy for over thirty-five years, and they have two adult children and two grandchildren.

NICOLE MARTIN

Reverend Doctor Nicole Massie Martin was born and educated in Baltimore, Maryland. She graduated magna cum laude from Vanderbilt University with a triple major in Human and Organizational Development, Educational Studies, and French. Dr. Martin received her Master of Divinity from Princeton Theological Seminary and earned a Doctor of Ministry from Gordon-Conwell Theological Seminary.

Dr. Martin serves as the Chief Operating Officer at Christianity Today. She is the founder and Executive Director of Soulfire International Ministries, which accelerates thriving for pastors, churches, and younger leaders. She is also active in her local congregation in Maryland at Kingdom Fellowship AME Church where she leads the Grow Ministry.

Dr. Martin is a gifted writer and author of numerous articles including three books: *Nailing It: Why Successful Leadership Demands Suffering & Surrender, Made to Lead: Empowering Women for Ministry and Leaning In, Letting Go: A Lenten Devotional*. She serves on the executive council of the National Association of Evangelicals, the board of trustees at Fuller Theological Seminary, and on the National Advisory Council for the Salvation Army. She is a founding board member of the Center for Christianity and

Public Life and has been inducted into the esteemed Board of Preachers at Morehouse College.

Dr. Martin is married to her best friend, Dr. Mark Martin, and they have two amazing daughters.

TERRY PARKMAN

@TERRYPARKMAN
TERRYPARKMAN.COM

Terry Parkman is the Global Lead for Empowered21 NextGen and the Global NextGen Ambassador for OneHope, helping raise up Spirit-empowered leaders around the world. He also serves as the Global Ministries Pastor at River Valley Church in Minneapolis, where he oversees missions, leadership, and global expansion. With over 20 years in ministry and a doctorate in Missiology, Terry is passionate about seeing the next generation step into their God-given purpose.

He lives in Minneapolis MN with his wife, Christina, and their daughters, Avalie and Nova.

VINCE PARKER

Vince Parker is the Senior Central Ministry Leader for Youth and Internships at Life. Church, where he's been shaping the next generation of leaders for 16 years. A visionary with a heart for empowering youth pastors, ministry strategists, and leaders worldwide, Vince is passionate about helping others boldly pursue Jesus and take faith-filled risks. He's a dedicated husband to Melissa, proud father to Adriana, self-proclaimed lawn care legend, and—most recently—a marathoner.

With over a decade and a half of experience, Vince is committed to equipping church leaders to go further, run harder, and build the Kingdom with endurance and unwavering faith.

ABOUT THE AUTHOR

Jurie Kriel serves on the senior leadership team of Shoreline Church in Austin, Texas, and leads NXT Move, a global initiative dedicated to mobilizing Christian leaders to accelerate Christianity in the next generation. Recognizing duplication and siloed thinking as major barriers to fulfilling the Great Commission, Jurie also serves as the Global Director for Collaboration with the Lausanne Movement, where he champions unified, strategic action across the global Church.

In Texas, Jurie previously served as Pastor for Preaching at Hill Country Bible Church and planted a church in Austin's urban core. Prior to his move to the U.S., he led and planted multiple campuses with Doxa Deo in South Africa and co-founded the Timothy Ministry Training Seminary, which continues to equip leaders serving in ministry around the world.

An experienced communicator and leadership consultant, Jurie has preached and facilitated strategic change in 46 U.S. states and 47 countries across every inhabited continent. He and his wife, Karin, have been joyfully married for 25 years and are proud parents to two sons, Joshua and Ethan.

JURIEKRIEL.COM

@JURIEKRIEL

NXTMOVE.GLOBAL

NOTES

CHAPTER 1: PIONEERING THE FUTURE

1. National Baseball Hall of Fame and Museum. (n.d.). Ted Williams goes 6-for-8. Baseball Hall of Fame. https://baseballhall.org/discover/inside-pitch/ted-williams-goes-6-for-8

2. Asbury, C. (2023). Pioneer [Song]. On Pioneer. Bethel Music. https://open.spotify.com/track/3vlEonKWGz9FwZxPjBh1cB

3. Lausanne Movement. (2024). The State of the Great Commission Report. https://lausanne.org/report

4. NXTMove. (2023, October). *Future of the Gospel Forum, World Evangelical Alliance (WEA).* Google Docs. https://docs.google.com/document/d/1yRIN2xHzjXGoipOBIDv4BVvrFwIU4-Vy/edit?usp=share_link&ouid=105306927238043728439&rtpof=true&sd=true

5. International Council for Evangelical Theological Education. (2023). ICETE C-25 Consultation – Tirana. https://icete.info/event/icete-c-25-tirana/

6. NXT Move Global. (2025). Home. https://www.nxtmove.global/

7. Hancock, T., & Bezold, C. (1994). Possible futures, preferable futures. The Healthcare Forum Journal, 37(2), 23–29.

CHAPTER 2: HITTING THE BALL YOU CANNOT SEE

1. Performance Vision. (n.d.). How is a fastball seen by baseball players? Performance Vision Inc. Retrieved May 5, 2025, from https://www.performancevisioninc.com/blog/41/how-is-a-fastball-seen-by-baseball-players/

2. Fuller, R. B. (1981). Critical path. St. Martin's Press.

3. Schilling, D. R. (2013, April 19). Knowledge doubling every 12 months, soon to be every 12 hours. Industry Tap. https://www.industrytap.com/knowledge-doubling-every-12-months-soon-to-be-every-12-hours/3950

4. Brinker, S. (2013, July 29). Martec's Law: Technology changes exponentially, organizations change logarithmically. Chief Marketing Technologist. https://chiefmartec.com/2013/07/martecs-law/

5. Nieuwhof, C. (2018). Didn't see it coming: Overcoming the seven greatest challenges that no one expects and everyone experiences. WaterBrook.

6. Whitehead, J. L., & Graham, M. J. (2023). The Great Dechurching: Who's leaving, why are they going, and what will it take to bring them back? Zondervan.

7. Drucker, P. F. (2007). *Innovation and entrepreneurship: Practice and principles.* HarperBusiness.

CHAPTER 3: SHIFTING DEFINITION OF BEING HUMAN

1. Apple Inc. (2007, January 9). Apple reinvents the phone with iPhone. Apple Newsroom. https://www.apple.com/newsroom/2007/01/09Apple-Reinvents-the-Phone-with-iPhone/

2. NVIDIA. (2024, March 18). NVIDIA Blackwell platform arrives to power a new era of computing. NVIDIA Newsroom. https://nvidianews.nvidia.com/news/nvidia-blackwell-platform-arrives-to-power-a-new-era-of-computing

3. Alcala, N. (2023, June 8). City Hall raises two Pride flags. Spartan Daily. https://sjsunews.com/article/city-hall-raises-two-pride-flags

4. University of California, Berkeley. (2025). Jennifer Doudna. Berkeley Research. https://vcresearch.berkeley.edu/faculty/jennifer-doudna

5. Costanza-Chock, S. (2020). Intersectional design cards. Stanford University Press. https://www.sup.org/books/sociology/intersectional-design-cards

6. Lausanne Movement. (2024). The State of the Great Commission Report. https://lausanne.org/report

7. Transhumanism | EBSCO Research Starters, accessed on August 13, 2025, https://www.ebsco.com/research-starters/social-sciences-and-humanities/transhumanism

8. Cole Stryker & Mark Scapicchio. (2024, March 22). *What is Generative AI?* IBM Think. Retrieved from https://www.ibm.com/think/topics/generative-ai

9. Amazon Web Services. (2025). *What is a GAN? Definition of Generative AI Network.* AWS. Retrieved August 13, 2025, from https://aws.amazon.com/what-is/gan/

CHAPTER 4: SHIFTING DELINEATIONS OF DIGITAL EXISTENCE

1. Berg, E. C. (2024, June 2). A Brazilian tribe is split by Elon Musk's Starlink. The New York Times. https://www.nytimes.com/2024/06/02/world/americas/starlink-internet-elon-musk-brazil-amazon.html

2. Brewminate. (2019, June 11). *Young and old: Examining the Strauss–Howe historiographical generations hypothesis.* https://brewminate.com/young-and-old-examining-the-strauss-howe-historiographical-generations-hypothesis/

3. Leyden, P. [Peter Leyden]. (2023, February 10). 2025: The end of the world as we know it [Video]. YouTube. https://www.youtube.com/watch?v=-zoCpFfOH04

4. Morgan Stanley. (2024, March 13). *The rise of humanoid robots: A conversation with Adam Jonas* [Video]. https://www.morganstanley.com/insights/videos/humanoid-robots-adam-jonas

5. NVIDIA. (2025). *Embodied AI.* https://www.nvidia.com/en-us/glossary/embodied-ai/

6. Meta. (2025). Emerging technology at Meta. https://www.meta.com/emerging-tech/

7. Yoon, J. (2022, March 6). Paying attention: The attention economy. Berkeley Economic Review. **https://econreview.studentorg.berkeley.edu/paying-attention-the-attention-economy/**

8. Davenport, T. H., & Beck, J. C. (2002). The attention economy: Understanding the new currency of business. Harvard Business School Press.

9. Blair, L. (2024, March 14). U.S. Bible sales boom as Gen Z turns to the physical Word. WORLD News Group. **https://wng.org/sift/u-s-bible-sales-boom-as-gen-z-turns-to-the-physical-word-1733353677**

10. Community of Christ – Greater Pacific Northwest USA Mission Center. (2023, July 17). The clash of generations: Church leadership. **https://cofchrist-gpnw.org/blog/the-clash-of-generations-church-leadership/**

11. Safari Memories. (n.d.). Masai Mara – Unique Safaris in Kenya. Safari-Memories. Retrieved August 13, 2025, from https://www.safari-memories.com/en/destinations/kenya/masai-mara#:~:text=The%20Masai%20Mara%20is%20the,during%20the%20long%20dry%20season.

12. Norton. (2021). *Digital generations: How different age groups interact with the online world.* **https://us.norton.com/blog/how-to/digital-generations**

12. Hawk-Eye Innovations. (2025). Official website. **https://www.hawkeyeinnovations.com/**

CHAPTER 5: SHIFTING DYNAMICS OF TRUST

1. Gharib, M. (2011, July 30). The theft that made the Mona Lisa a masterpiece. NPR. **https://www.npr.org/2011/07/30/138800110/the-theft-that-made-the-mona-lisa-a-masterpiece**

2. Dixit, A. K., & Weibull, J. W. (2007). Political polarization. Proceedings of the National Academy of Sciences, 104(18), 7351–7356. **https://doi.org/10.1073/pnas.0702071104**

3. Brenan, M. (2023, October 16). *Americans' trust in media remains near record low. Gallup.* **https://news.gallup.com/poll/651977/americans-trust-media-remains-trend-low.aspx**

4. Levine, T. R. (2022). Truth-default theory 20 years later: A brief review, update, and commentary. Human Communication Research, 48(3), 343–353. **https://doi.org/10.1093/hcr/hqac012**

5. Business Infographics. (2024, March 7). How psychological safety is related to performance [Infographic]. LinkedIn. **https://www.linkedin.com/posts/business-infographics_how-psychological-safety-related-to-performance-activity-7157492539824979968-sWCU**

CHAPTER 6: SHIFTING DIMENSIONS OF ORGANIZATION

1. Bolsinger, T. (2015). *Canoeing the mountains: Christian leadership in uncharted territory.* InterVarsity Press.

2. Groch, I. (2023, February 28). *The rise and fall of Blockbuster: A detailed account. Medium.* https://medium.com/@igorgrochu/the-rise-and-fall-of-blockbuster-a-detailed-account-11324a49acd9

3. VdoCipher. (2017, June 16). *The Netflix revolution – Part 1: History of Netflix.* https://www.vdocipher.com/blog/2017/06/netflix-revolution-part-1-history/

4. Practical Theology Today. (2024, January 4). *Dietrich Bonhoeffer quotes.* https://practicaltheologytoday.com/2024/01/04/dietrich-bonhoeffer-quotes/[Content includes quotes commonly attributed to Bonhoeffer, though original authorship is unverified.]

5. McCarthy, J. (2023, January 16). *The richest 1% own almost two-thirds of global wealth, Oxfam says. Global Citizen.* https://www.globalcitizen.org/en/content/wealth-inequality-oxfam-billionaires-elon-musk/

6. Adidas Group. (2016, May 24). *Adidas' first SPEEDFACTORY lands in Germany.* https://www.adidas-group.com/en/media/press-releases/adidas-first-speedfactory-lands-in-germany

7. Keating, J. (2017, April 20). *Speed wins. Eurobiz Japan.* https://eurobiz.jp/feature/speed-wins/

8. McChrystal Group. (2025). *How becoming a Team of Teams helps organizations thrive.* https://www.mcchrystalgroup.com/#:~:text=How%20becoming%20a%20Team%20of,for%20100+%20organizations%20across%20industries.

9. McChrystal Group. (2025). *Shared consciousness.* McChrystal Group. https://www.mcchrystalgroup.com/capabilities/team-of-teams/shared-consciousness

10. EM360 Tech. (2023, August 15). *What happened to Blockbuster? How streaming killed the video store.* https://em360tech.com/tech-articles/what-happened-blockbuster-how-streaming-killed-video-store

CHAPTER 7: SHIFTING DEGREES OF SEPARATION

1. Milgram, S. (1967). The small world problem. Psychology Today, 2(1), 60–67.

2. Wikipedia contributors. (n.d.). *SixDegrees.com.* Wikipedia. Retrieved June 27, 2025, from https://en.wikipedia.org/wiki/SixDegrees.com

3. Favs HQ. (2025). *The genesis of social media: A look back at Six Degrees.* Retrieved June 27, 2025, from https://favshq.com/blog/the-genesis-of-social-media-a-look-back-at-six-degrees

4. Facebook Research. (2016, February 4). *Three and a half degrees of separation.* https://research.facebook.com/blog/2016/2/three-and-a-half-degrees-of-separation/

5. Matejuk, K. (2021, March 6). *Complete analysis of the network of my LinkedIn connections. Medium.* https://medium.com/@kamilmatejuk/complete-analysis-of-the-network-of-my-linkedin-connections-169d1c7d9ff6

6. University of Michigan. (2022, December 13). *The loneliness paradox: How media narratives shape our solitude.* https://news.umich.edu/the-loneliness-paradox-how-media-narratives-shape-our-solitude/

7. Sakamoto, S., & Nagaoka, M. (2025). Psychological factors related to social exclusion of Hikikomori (prolonged social withdrawal) individuals by local residents. *The Japanese Journal of Health and Human Ecology*. Advance online publication. **https://www.jstage.jst.go.jp/article/yam/advpub/0/advpub_2025.05.011/_article**

8. Asia Pacific Foundation of Canada. (2023, April 6). *2% of Japanese labour force could be 'modern-day recluses': Government survey.* **https://www.asiapacific.ca/publication/2-percent-japanese-labour-force-modern-day-recluses**

9. Cameron, B. (2023, April 4). *Why young women are leaving the church in droves. Medium.* **https://medium.com/backyard-theology/why-young-women-are-leaving-the-church-in-droves-d4a3066dfccc**

10. Miami Premier Padel. (2023, December 28). *Padel, a global phenomenon in continuous expansion: Played on 70,000 courts across 150 countries.* **https://www.miamipremierpadel.com/padel-a-global-phenomenon-in-continuous-expansion-played-on-70000-courts-across-150-countries**

CHAPTER 8: SHIFTING DISCOVERY OF BELONGING

1. Oldenburg, R. (1997). The great good place: Cafés, coffee shops, bookstores, bars, hair salons, and other hangouts at the heart of a community (2nd ed.). Marlowe & Company. **https://raggeduniversity.co.uk/wp-content/uploads/2025/03/1_x_The-Great-Good-Place-Cafes-Coffee-Shops-Bookstores-Bars-Ray-Oldenburg-.pdf**

2. World Health Organization. (2025, June 30). *Social connection linked to improved health and reduced risk of early death.* **https://www.who.int/news/item/30-06-2025-social-connection-linked-to-improved-heath-and-reduced-risk-of-early-death**

3. Murthy, V. H. (2022). The U.S. Surgeon General's advisory on the healing effects of social connection and community. *JAMA Psychiatry, 79*(10), 933–934. **https://doi.org/10.1001/jamapsychiatry.2022.2225**

4. Sustainability Directory. (2025). What role does sustainable lifestyle play in longevity? **https://lifestyle.sustainability-directory.com/question/what-role-does-sustainable-lifestyle-play-in-longevity/**

5. Ballard Brief. (2023). *Isolation among Generation Z in the United States.* **https://ballardbrief.byu.edu/issue-briefs/isolation-among-generation-z-in-the-united-states**

6. Pew Research Center. (2023, March 28). How the pandemic has affected attendance at U.S. religious services. **https://www.pewresearch.org/religion/2023/03/28/how-the-pandemic-has-affected-attendance-at-u-s-religious-services/**

7. Sketchplanations. (2024). Chickens and pigs. **https://sketchplanations.com/chickens-and-pigs**

8. Thomas, G. (2010). Sacred pathways: Discover your soul's path to God. Zondervan. **https://www.amazon.com/Sacred-Pathways-Discover-Your-Souls/dp/0310329884**

9. U.S. Department of Health and Human Services. (2023). *Our epidemic of loneliness and isolation: The U.S. Surgeon General's advisory on the healing effects of social connection and community.* https://www.hhs.gov/sites/default/files/surgeon-general-social-connection-advisory.pdf

CHAPTER 9: TOWARD 2050

1. American Chemical Society. (2025). Discovery and development of penicillin. https://www.acs.org/education/whatischemistry/landmarks/flemingpenicillin.html

2. SCRUMstudy. (June 09, 2024). Agile Scrum: Adaptation to change. https://www.scrumstudy.com/article/agile-scrum-adaptation-to-change

3. Department of Justice and Constitutional Development, Republic of South Africa. (2025). *Truth and Reconciliation Commission (TRC).* https://www.justice.gov.za/trc/

4. BBC News. (2024, January 4). *Teen arrested for "swatting" gamer during livestream.* https://www.bbc.com/news/world-us-canada-67871775

5. Wild, J. (2023, December 29). *AI plays Tetris so well it breaks the game. Game Rant.* https://gamerant.com/ai-plays-tetris-so-well-it-breaks-the-game/